Baking Through My Brokenness

Kim Elizabeth Russell

Baking Through My Brokenness
Copyright © 2016 Kim Elizabeth Russell

All rights reserved. No part of this book may be used or reproduced by any means, graphic, electronic, or mechanical, including photocopying, recording, taping or by any information storage retrieval system, without the written permission of the publisher except in the case of brief quotations embodied in critical articles and reviews.

Entegrity Choice Publishing
PO Box 453
Powder Springs, GA 30127
info@entegritypublishing.com

The views expressed in this work are solely those of the author and do not necessarily reflect the views of the publisher, and the publisher hereby disclaims any responsibility for them.

This is a work of fiction. All of the characters, names, incidents, organizations and dialogue in this novel are either products of the author's imagination or are used fictitiously.

Book Cover Designed by:
Kylie Dalton

ISBN: 978-0-9974859-1-2
ISBN: 978-0-9974859-2-9 (eBook)

Library of Congress Control Number: 2016938186

Printed in the United States of America

Acknowledgements

I give honor to the Most High God, the Lord and savior of my life. I bless Your Name, Jehovah-Rapha, my Healer and the One who makes bitter experiences sweet. You sent your Word to heal me and rescue me from the darkness. You forgave me for all of my iniquities and healed all of my diseases.

To my amazing, loving, and supportive sons, Ron Powell and Dre Russell, thank you for inspiring me to tell my story. When I made the decision to publish my life journey, you cheered me forward.

I would like to thank Roxie Hairston, my awesome Publisher, who did not allow me to become discouraged.

Many thanks to my friends Renee' Beckford, Veronica Womack, Tammy Traylor, Yolanda Jenkins, and Pamela Bynum. Renee' Beckford, my cousin, sister, and best friend, for providing immeasurable love and support. Veronica Womack, my best friend since middle school, for displaying astonishing confidence in me. Tammy Traylor, my good dear friend, for reviewing my rough drafts, and providing honest feedback for me to tell my story as if I was reading it for the first time. Yolanda Jenkins, my friend, mentor, and prayer intercessor. Pamela Bynum, thank you for critiquing the first draft of my manuscript, and motivating me to start over and tell my truth.

Dedication

This book is dedicated to my grandparents; the late Mr. Henry and Josephine Powell and Mr. Bobby and Mrs. Annie Eashmon, who saved my life. Thank you for teaching me the things I needed to know as a Woman and Mother. Thank you for teaching me how to cook and bake for my family and for teaching me that I will never be too old to learn; and "don't put off until tomorrow what you can do today - tomorrow is not promised."

Thank you Annie Eashmon (my maternal grandmother) for stepping up to be the grandmother I so desperately needed. Thank you for your words of wisdom and for loving me.

Thank you Uncle Charles, I love and miss you. You will forever be in my heart.

Thank you Aunt Sandra for all of your love, support and prayers. When things got tough you were there for me and my children. I will thank God for you as long as I live.

Contents

The Beginning 13
Chocolate Swirl Pound Cake

The Family 17
Butter Pound Cake

Why Do I Need Adopting? 21
Triple Berry Scone

Dear Diary 27
Oreo Cheesecake

Willie Guess What? 35
Strawberry Cake

Not Again 41
Caramel Cake

Catch Me Please 47
Sock-It-To-Me Cake

Mr. & Mrs. Did Others 55
Red Velvet Cake

You Better Not Hit My Mother 67
Devil's Food Cheesecake

There Is Nothing Sweet Here 77
Coconut Cake

Black Forest Cake 83
Turn on the Lights

Kimmie Kakes & Things 91

Author's Note

Baking Through My Brokenness allows me the chance to share my passion of baking that gave me therapeutic solace during my most difficult trials. The kitchen has been my favorite room in the house since childhood. Mixing frosting and layering cakes was one of my favorite healing pass times. I share some of my beloved baking recipes in the chapter titled, "Kimmie Kakes & Things."

Introduction

I recall having a conversation with a friend eight years ago about writing a book about my life. Numerous times I shared my story with girlfriends and the replies were always the same; "You should write a book."

At last, I found the strength and courage to put my life "out there." A lot of painful memories reemerged as I wrote my story however, I found a release of healing and victory as I began to realize that I made it through the sting of deception and disappointment.

Within these pages, my story of triumph is exposed and God is exalted. For years, I was in a dark manhole. There is no other way to describe the pain. Everything around me was dark. Depression gripped me and would not let me go. I searched desperately for light but I could not find my way to the light until God removed what felt like a hundred pound weight sinking my soul deep into despair.

I love and adore the Most High God, he gave me his only begotten son to save my life. I found blessed assurance in God; God is my Father, God is my Healer, God is my Banner, God is my Friend and He is my all in all.

The devil thought he had crippled me for life but through the resurrected Savior, I found hope and now live the abundant life through Jesus Christ.

Chapter 1

The Beginning

Chocolate Swirl Pound Cake

As I prepare to bake this chocolate, sweet, decadent pound cake, I think of my life. This cake resembles my dark complexion, and the muddy mixture represents the dark and dense secrets of my twirl and twisted life.

As a child, my favorite treat was Jack's coconut cookies. You could get two for a penny at the Lil' General Store. My warmest memory in buying the cookies is my Daddy lifting me up, so that I could reach the counter to get the cookies from that clear container with the red lid.

Thinking about the Lil' General Store brings back memories of my childhood in Tampa, Florida. I grew up in a "shotgun" house. For those who don't know what a shotgun house is, it is a house in which one could stand on the front porch and see straight through to the backyard. In a shotgun house, there were no closets. A closet consisted of poles erected in the corners of the rooms to hang clothes.

My parents didn't have a lot of money but we always had a hot meal and clean clothes. Speaking of clean clothes, I fondly remember whenever the washing machine was not working or momma couldn't get to the laundromat, she washed our clothes on a washboard. The dryer consisted of a clothesline erected with 2x4's and rope in the backyard.

Daddy worked as a steel cutter for the largest steel company in Tampa. I vividly recall a time when the three owners, Mr. McCullum, Mr. Simpson and Mr. Anderson were proud of my dad for taking a firm stance against joining his co-workers on a steel strike. He was uncompromising in his position and the 20-30 holes riddled in the wall of our house was evidence. On the night that the house got shot up, a car was heard pulling up to the house and then before anyone could see who it was, a sudden barrage of bullets ricocheted through the house. Daddy summoned everyone to get under the beds to avoid getting hit. Thankfully, no one was harmed from the incident. Daddy's decision not to strike made a huge impact on the owners of the company. Fifteen years after his retirement, the owners awarded him with a medal for his dedication and loyal service.

Momma worked as a maid for a prominent lumber business owner in an upscale neighborhood in Tampa. She wore the same type of maid dress that Alice wore on the Brady Bunch. Sometimes she had to stay overnight on the job if there was a big party or if the couple was out of town. When her workday ended, she headed home to cook and clean for us.

The rest of the family clan included brothers, Raymond, Willie, Leroy, Clarence and my sister, Sonia. When Willie, Leroy and Clarence graduated from high school, they joined the military. Sonia married her high school sweetheart and moved to North Carolina. My brother Raymond and I were the only ones left at home.

Sonia and I were very close and her move out of state was devastating. I cried for days after she left. She promised to check on me and she did. When my mom would shout, "Sonia is on the phone," I dropped everything and ran as fast as I could to get to the phone. My first words were, "I miss you."

"I love you and I miss you, Kim," She would immediately say. Before the call ended, Sonia always said, "Kim, be a good little girl for Momma and Daddy. I will see you soon." Once the conversation ended, I gave the phone back to Momma and I ran to tell my dolls that my sister called and she said that she loves me.

When Raymond wanted to get under my skin, he would tell me that my parents found me and brought me home. Afterwards, he would laugh hysterically and I would cry.

Raymond frequently teased me with the "we found you" story. According to Raymond, my parents were driving from Aunt Candy's house, crossing over the Cass Street Bridge and saw a baby wrapped in a blanket. Daddy stopped the car and Momma jumped out and picked the baby up. After searching and finding no one to claim the baby, they brought me home. He said my diaper smelled something awful. He always ended the story laughing hysterically and I cried.

One night Momma overheard Raymond telling the "we found you" story and she yelled, "Stop telling her that lie, Raymond. Kim, we drove you home from the hospital." Momma then told me to get ready for bed because tomorrow was "Picture Day"

"Picture day?" I repeated.

Skipping down the hallway to my room, Daddy followed to make sure I said my prayers before bed. Once in my room, our knees hit the floor and Daddy began praying; "Now I lay me down to sleep, I pray the Lord my soul to keep. If I should die before I wake, I pray the Lord my soul to take, Amen."

The next morning, I was dreaming when I heard Momma yell, "Kim! Kimmie, wake up." I heard her, but I couldn't move.

"Run, Kim," I was yelling to myself.

I was running, waving and screaming trying to get away from flying bugs. I could not out run them and the more I ran and waved them away, they appeared to multiply. I was calling for my momma but she didn't answer. I felt alone with no one to protect me from the flying bugs. As I started to cry, I heard Momma say, "Kim, wake up. It's me; wake up."

Slowly I awoke from sleep. Momma picked me up and held me tight.

"You were having a bad dream," She kept saying.

After I calmed down from the bad dream, Momma put me down and got ready for school. Shortly, she returned with a comb, brush and a jar of Royal Crown hair grease. I couldn't wait for Momma to finish my hair. I was excited to put on my new green dress, white trimmed lace socks and my black patent leather shoes for picture day.

When the doorbell rang, I jumped for joy to see Ms. Washington. As I reached for the door knob, Mom appeared with a Polaroid camera in her hand yelling.

"Wait, I want a picture."

Ms. Washington, the headmaster at Washington's Daycare, picked me up every day for school.

Down the front porch steps, I went with Ms. Washington and jumped into her white, 1963 Oldsmobile 88 station wagon. Inside the car, I remembered I didn't kiss Momma goodbye, so I ran back to kiss her. As I ran back outside, Ms. Washington was holding the car door open and motioned me to climb into the back seat. It was picture day, and I was the happiest five year old on Cypress Street.

It seemed forever for my pictures to come back from "Picture Day." Each day I saw Ms. Washington, I asked about the pictures and she would say, "Not today Kim; they are not ready."

"I have a surprise for you; your pictures are here," Ms. Washington said as I was climbing into the car one more. Finally.

When Ms. Washington dropped me off at home after school, I ran into the house with my pictures yelling "Momma! Daddy, I got my pictures!" My parents were not home, but Grandma Alice was there.

"Stop running in the house, little girl," She yelled. Grandma Alice was always around when Momma or Daddy wasn't going to be at home.

My pictures were beautiful, and I couldn't wait to show them to my parents. As I was sitting down on the sofa waiting for them to come home, I fell asleep. Suddenly, I heard Momma talking but I did not see her. I thought I woke up, but then I realized that I couldn't move. Again, I heard voices and someone saying, "Kim is sleep; I don't want to wake her from her nap." I wanted to jump up so badly and say I am here but I couldn't move or talk. Slowly, tears began rolling down my face so I closed my eyes real tight and when I opened them, I screamed and Grandma came running. I jumped up from the sofa and grabbed her around the waist. When I stopped crying she said, "If that monster mess with you again, I will hit it in the head and throw it in the backyard for the trash man to pick-up."

This is the beginning......

Chapter 2

The Family

Butter Pound Cake

Family was very important to my family. Every Saturday night my Mother would take the butter from the refrigerator to sit out overnight. When we made it home from church, she would set all the ingredients on the table; mix and fold, then pour the sweet smelling batter into an old fashion Dutch Oven; she would gently slide it in the oven; when the cake was a beautiful golden brown, she removed it from the oven to cool; she flipped that cake onto a plate and covered it with a kitchen towel until the unveiling. I anticipated licking the batter from the mixing bowl when she offered it to me.

Momma was hastily preparing a big Sunday dinner for my sister, Sonia and her husband, Jarrod. They were coming home to stay for a spell with their new baby. Momma made her famous fried chicken, pot roast, turnip greens with the roots, rice, potato salad, corn bread and for dessert, her famous butter pound cake for the homecoming.

Family members were arriving one by one. Everyone was anxiously waiting to see Sonia, Jarrod and the new baby.

"They are here," someone yelled and we all ran outside and stood on the front porch.

"She's here," I yelled, jumping up and down. Sonia and her family maneuvered through the welcome line. There were lots of hugs and kisses; everyone was happy to see Sonia.

"Kim, come meet your niece, Olivia," Sonia said, once they were all inside the house. She also announced that Jarrod was leaving in a few days to take care of business with his job but did not offer any other details.

Everyone was getting pretty hungry so Dad said, "enough talking; it's time to eat." Daddy blessed the food and then began singing "Won't It Be Grand" while everyone proceeded through the buffet line.

Later that night after everyone was gone, Daddy asked me to bring him his Prince Albert tobacco and turn the television on, so he could watch the L.A. Dodgers and the Pittsburg Pirates game.

I was planning on staying up awhile with Daddy but Momma yelled, "Kim, get ready for bed." After putting on my PJs, I knelt down to repeat my regular prayer.

"Now I lay me down to sleep, I pray the Lord my soul to keep. If I should die before I wake, I pray the Lord my soul to take. And God, thank you for Sonia, Jarrod and my new niece Olivia, Amen."

The next morning, I heard Dad ask Sonia how long Jarrod will be gone.

"You have me and your grand-daughter for a year," she replied.

Mom entered the kitchen and told Sonia about a High School Reunion Dance that is being held at school tonight. Sonia was thrilled and yelled, "Clarence and I are going and we will enter the dance contest and win." An excited Sonia grabbed my hand and began to do the two-step dance, spinning me around.

"Raymond, I need you to watch Kim and Olivia," Sonia said.

"Why," asked Raymond?

"Mom is going out with Aunt Lillie and Dad just walked out the back door on his way to Mr. Fred's house."

Baking Through My Brokenness

Mom always fussed whenever Dad went to Mr. Fred's house, because he undoubtedly would drink too much and come home in a cussing or fighting mood. Mr. Fred lived at the end of our street. You could always see Mr. Fred walking down the street wearing a dark brown fedora with sweat rings around the brim. He appeared to be a nice man. You could often see his chickens and roosters pecking in the back yard.

Mr. Fred liked to scare me. He knew that I was afraid of the black and red grasshoppers and for that matter, the yellow ones too.

"Watch out Kim! The grasshoppers can fly." At his taunting, I would take off running toward home crying all the way.

After Sonia and Raymond went back and forward regarding babysitting, Raymond finally resigned that he would be the babysitter for the night.

Raymond didn't want to do much babysitting, so he told me to go to bed. I didn't mind that too much because I was excited to put on my new pink and white pajamas that Sonia bought me. She also bought a pair for Olivia; we were dressed like twins.

Olivia fell asleep in her crib in the corner of the room, and I fell asleep in the bed next to her crib. Across the room, Raymond laid on top of the bed watching TV.

Once I fell asleep, I began to dream about big bugs and spiders chasing me and I was frantically trying to run away. Sonia returned home before Clarence with their first place trophy from the Dance Contest.

Suddenly, I was awakened from the dream by a piercing scream. When I jumped out of bed, I saw Sonia standing near the crib screaming and crying. She picked Olivia up, held her in her arms and fell to the floor. Sonia's scream was so loud that Clarence heard it from a block away. Clarence ran toward the direction of the scream. When he arrived home, he found his sister distraught.

In the chaos, I searched for Raymond and found him sitting on the edge of the bed with his head in his hands crying. What happened, I thought to myself.

"What's wrong with my sister and my niece?" I don't remember speaking, moving or crying.

Olivia suffocated. Raymond carried the guilt of Olivia's death with him for many years and even now, he may be trying to deal with it.

My little niece died that night; she left us to go be with God. My sister and her husband lost their baby daughter; my momma and daddy lost their granddaughter; and my brothers lost their niece.

How did we deal with it? Who is blaming themselves? It wasn't anyone's fault.

Olivia was a happy baby. I can see her smile as I am writing this story. She was a chunky, milk chocolate baby with pudgy cheeks. She will never be forgotten...

RIP my little niece.

Chapter 3

Why Do I Need Adopting?

Triple Berry Scone

I was sitting at the kitchenette sipping on coffee, breaking off the corners of my warm mixed berry scone; watching the hummingbird fly back and forth by the kitchen window. I was missing what I never had with my birth mother, "The Berry Bond." For years, I wrestled to understand why my mother gave me away. I want to know who made the decision to give me away and why.

"Happy Birthday Kim, how old are you?" Momma asked?

"I am nine years old."

I couldn't wait to rip the paper off of my Twist and Turn Julia Doll. Each time I watched the Diahann Carroll television show, I sat my doll on the table and we watched the show together.

As I was opening my gifts, mom told me to hurry because we had to go downtown. "Can I take my doll with me?"

"Yes, put on your blue dress and a slip. We need to hurry; we can't be late."

"Why are we going downtown? Who are we going to see?" I asked.

"A man about a cow," Dad yelled.

"We're going to get a cow?" I asked.

I guess I was too young to understand the where, because my next question would have been why. In my mind, there were only two reasons to go downtown: business or shopping.

Sonia dropped us off in front of a tall building downtown. After riding the elevator, we went into a room filled with brown furniture. I sat in a large cold chair at a long rectangle shaped table and a man and a lady walked in smiling.

"It is always good to see you again, Mr. Henry," the man said. Daddy shook his hand and the man hugged Momma.

"Now I need to talk with Kim. You can sit out in the waiting area."

"Kim, my name is Mr. Judge. What is the name of your doll?"

"Her name is Julia, she's on TV."

"Kim, I would like to get to know you. I would like to talk about how you like living with your momma and daddy.

"Kim, do you like the school you attend" he asked.

"I like my school and my teacher" I answered.

"How do you like your momma's cooking" he asked?

"I love Momma's cooking. She cooks for my friend Keebler and his family."

"What is your favorite food?"

I stood up and rubbed my tummy.

"My momma's fried chicken is the best in the world. I will ask my momma and daddy if you can come over for dinner."

Mr. Judge started laughing, got up and called my momma back into the room.

"Mrs. Josephine, Kim is a happy little girl; she is in good hands. My secretary will give you the next step in the process. Thank you for coming."

We went home after meeting. Mr. Judge and no one ever mentioned him again.

The next winter, I woke up to Momma shaking me.

"Kim, wake up, wake up; you stopped breathing."

For as long as I can remember, I got sick with a high fever every winter break. Most often, Momma's cold home remedy (grapefruit juice, sugar and kerosene) cured me. It was a nasty tasting medicine, but it made me feel better.

After swallowing the nasty medicine, Momma rubbed me down with Vick's Vapor rub and wrapped in layers of blankets. When I woke the next morning, my pajamas were wet and the fever was worse. Momma was alarmed and asked my aunt to take us to the hospital.

After I was examined, the doctors performed an emergency tonsillectomy and adenoidectomy. The doctor told my momma if she had waited another 24-48 hours to bring me to the hospital, I would have died in my sleep from suffocation.

In the Recovery Room, the nurse told me that I could only have ice cream or popsicles for seventy-two hours. Eating ice cream for three days was the best part of being sick.

I was soon released from the hospital. While sleeping on the sofa, after returning home from the hospital, Momma and Daddy approached me. I was a little dazed, slipping in and out of sleep. They sat on opposite ends of the sofa.

"We need to tell you something and what we are going to tell you does not mean that we don't love you," Momma said. When I looked into Daddy's face, there were tears rolling down his face, and I heard the sadness in Momma's voice.

"Willie is not your brother," Momma said. "Willie and Patricia are your real momma and daddy. Willie asked us to take care of you and raise you. Remember when we went downtown and you talked to that man in his office?"

'Yes ma'am, I talked with Mr. Judge."

Well, your daddy and I were trying to adopt you. And we still want to but Willie and Patricia insisted that you know the truth first.

"I don't want to live with them, please don't send me away, please, Daddy." I screamed.

"Can I still call you 'Momma'?" I asked.

'Yes,' she said. "You can call us Momma and Daddy!"

In the meantime, Sonia called Willie and told him that I had emergency surgery and they were on their way to see me. When they arrived, Momma told them that I knew the truth but I want to stay with them.

When Willie and Patricia came into the house, they walked up to me and began looking me over. Suddenly, a wave of anger rose up in me and their presence made me sick. I wanted them to leave. I was so angry that I rolled over and went to sleep. I prayed that they would be gone when I woke up.

No such luck. They were still there when I woke up. They had some nerve sitting at my momma's table eating our food. I wanted to get up and shout so that everyone on Cypress Street could hear me say, "I Hate You, Willie! And I Hate You Patricia!"

I refrained from the outburst because I knew that Momma would be angry if I did it. Nevertheless, I shouted it in my mind over and over until I fell asleep again.

The news that my brother Willie is my real father shattered my heart into a million pieces. I want to know when is a child's mind ready to comprehend admittance that the people she calls Momma and Daddy are not her birth parents. My heart ached and as I grew, so did my resentment toward everyone.

Some say that a child should not be told something so detrimental at a young age and others disagree. How was I supposed to handle this information? I have wrestled all of my life with this pain of rejection. It is true— hurt people hurt people.

I could not understand who made the decision to give me away and why. Who initiated the conversation? This is what I think was said during a conversation between Willie and Patricia on their wedding day when they decided to leave me behind.

> *Patricia: I can't wait to get home to get out of this wedding dress.*
> *Willie: Patricia, you know we need to do something with Kim, don't you?*
> *Patricia: Yeah Willie, I know. Can you not start that again; we just got married? Can I enjoy my day; thank you.*
> *Willie: This is your fault. If you hadn't messed around on me with that joker, we wouldn't be having this conversation.*
> *Patricia: I know, Willie, Give it a rest. I said I was sorry and it won't happen again. It was a one-time thing. Anyway, it's really your fault, I saw you talking to your ex-girlfriend in front of your Mother's house. So the way I see it, we are even. Don't start with me.*
> *Willie: Well, what are you going to do, because she can't come with us?*

Patricia: I know she can't; maybe my cousin Margaret or Aunt Lena will keep her until we come back for her. I need a cigarette. Have you seen my cigarette pouch?
Willie: I don't know when we are coming back or if I want to. Bad things seem to happen to me in Tampa.
Patricia: What? Willie, shut up talking like that. We have to come see our families. Maybe I can ask my sister to keep her.
Willie: You need to think of somebody because we already have a daughter (Yvette) and I hope you are pregnant, because I want a son.
Patricia: Willie, ask your parents if they would keep her until we come back for her.
Willie: You don't listen do you? I told you that I don't know when we will be back. I told them yesterday that she is not their granddaughter and now you want me to ask them if they would keep her, that's stupid.
Patricia: Ask them anyway. If they say no, I will just leave her with my momma but not without a fight. I told you about my son. He lives with his father's family. My momma did not want me to give him to them. That is why she most likely will say no if I ask her to keep Kim. I don't know why momma gets so upset about my decisions; she didn't raise me.
Willie: You never told me about a son. So you have three children?
Patricia: Willie H, I told you about my son and you said it didn't matter because you love me. You drink too much liquor; that's probably why you don't remember.

He dismissed her remarks.

Willie: Kim's jaundice is getting better; she will be released soon, and we need to have a plan. You should go to the hospital today to see your daughter.
Patricia: You are my husband, not my Daddy; I will go see her when I feel like it or I may never go. I know you told your family that Kim is not your child but they love her so, why don't we just ask them to keep her?

Chapter 4

Dear Diary

Oreo Cheesecake

Oreo cookies were a childhood treat. I would separate the dark cookies from the center to dip into a glass of milk and watch the cookies crumbs dissolve into the milk. Each layer of the cookie reminded me of how my life became twisted and separated from the center of my life.

Today is Friday. In gym class today, I saw a classmate writing in a little book, so I asked her about it. She said she was writing her secrets in her diary. Her little diary was pink and red with a lock and key. I didn't have any money to buy a diary like the one she had, so I made a diary. I took notebook paper and cut it in half and stapled the pages together while in art class that day. I don't have anyone to talk to, so I would write to my diary, because I know it will keep my secrets. These are the secrets I want you, my diary, to know.

First of all, my little cousin Olivia died; that's all I have to say about it. Today is Sunday and I fell asleep in church. Momma took me to the bathroom and reminded me of her promise that she will pop me in the mouth in front of everyone if I fell asleep in church.

Last year I was sent to New York to spend the summer with Willie and Patricia. I don't ever want to live with them. They argued everyday about me being there. I heard them talking about me staying with them forever. Willie said he wanted me to stay, but Patricia said maybe next summer. Patricia was mean. She said I was greedy and that I make her sick. I wanted to call Momma. I wanted to go home and never see them again; I hate them.

~ ~ ~

Today is Wednesday. I am scared of bugs, grasshoppers and spiders. I am scared to take naps or fall asleep in the daytime because when I try to get up, I can't move. My body won't move and nobody can hear me. I cannot see around the room and it scares me. At night, I am scared to go to the bathroom because of the big spiders on the wall by the bathroom. I got a beating last night because I peed in my clothes. I tried to tell Momma that the spider was going to jump on me, but she spanked me anyway.

~ ~ ~

Today is Monday. I think Toni (Olivia's sister) is sad because her daddy don't live with them anymore. Something happened to me when I spent the night with Sonia and Toni. I had to go over there because Momma was gone to Sarasota to gamble on the Jai-Alai games. After saying our prayers, Toni climbed into her bed and I got into the bed by the door. Suddenly, I felt something under my covers in my panties. I opened my eyes and there was a huge shadow on the side of the bed. I was scared. I couldn't move and the shadow man said "shhh." I just laid there on my back with my eyes closed. The huge shadow put his hands in my pajama bottoms touching me in that place. Momma said men do not touch little girls there but I didn't know why she said that. I couldn't see the shadow's face; I just saw the night light from the hallway.

The next day Sonia took me home. I was going to tell Momma but I didn't know how. I thought what if I would get in trouble or what if she hit me. Later that night after I said my prayers, I wondered what the shadow man was looking for in my panties. I pulled my pants from my stomach and looked into my panties; I couldn't see what the shadow man wanted in my panties.

Today is Saturday. I got a spanking for wetting the bed last night. I tried to get up and go to the bathroom but I was scared. Willie and Patricia called; I didn't want to talk to them.

Today is Sunday. Momma went to the dog track with Ms. Brown and Ms. Alice last night. I had to stay with Sonia and Toni. After we said our prayers, I checked the closet for the shadow man.

"What are you looking for?" Sonia asked.

"Nothing," I said.

That night, the shadow man entered the room again. I squeezed my eyes as tight as I could. I felt the shadow getting closer. I crossed my legs under the covers. He got on his knees next to my bed and lifted the cover up to slide his hands in my night clothes.

Diary, guess what happened? Suddenly out of nowhere; it was Wonder Woman. She came to save me from the shadow man. She kicked him in the back of his head, and then she slapped him to the ground. She kicked him again and then pulled him by his feet out of the room.

I heard the shadow man begging for her to stop hitting him with the baseball bat. I peeped through my eyes and saw flashing red and blue lights outside the bedroom window. I was scared; I prayed that Wonder Woman was ok. I squeezed my eyes tight praying that Sonia was safe from the shadow man. When I opened my eyes, Sonia was standing over me with tears in her eyes.

"Are you ok?" she asked. She hugged me tight and kissed me on my forehead. She said, "Come on. Let's say our prayers again.'

After we said our prayers I went back to sleep. I never saw the shadow man again.

Today is Monday. I don't like my school; I hate Momma and Daddy. We are poor; our lights were off yesterday because Daddy didn't pay the bill. Daddy drinks all the time and Momma is always gone to gamble so that she can win money to pay bills. My hair won't grow; my nose is really pointy, and I am black and ugly.

My junior high school English teacher, Ms. King pulled me aside one day to inform me that she had spoken to my grandmother about my attitude. She said that due to my circumstances at home, I had become belligerent.

"Kim, it is not your fault that your parents gave you to your grandmother; you cannot take it out on the world."

"Vivian, Gail and Paula have both of their parents," I said as I stood up, and pushed my chair back with force. I attempted to walk out of her office.

"Sit down, young lady, and I am only going to say it once," she said. Ms. King looked directly into my eye. "It is not your fault, little girl. Clear your head and your heart and go home. When you walk into my class tomorrow, you better have a good attitude."

~~~

Today is Tuesday. I heard Peaches talking to Shanae about cheerleading try-outs that were taking place in five days. I always wanted to be a cheerleader; I think. I don't know why, I just want to belong to something. I want to be a part of something. I want to be important to somebody. I needed a navy blue shirt, white socks and a white shirt for try-outs. I decided not to ask Momma for the money because I overheard her telling Aunt Lillie that she didn't have any money. I decided to put together my own uniform for the try-outs. I found a pair of old pants my Aunt Lillie gave me for Christmas last year. I cut the pants into shorts. I found a white shirt and borrowed a pair of Raymond's basketball socks.

~~~

Today is Friday. I didn't make the cheerleading squad. I knew that I wasn't going to make it. I tried to put my hair in a neat pony tail, but I couldn't because my hair wasn't long enough. All of the girls had their solid blue shorts, and their hair was in a pretty pony tail. I don't care anyway, I hate cheerleaders; I really didn't want to be with those girls.

~~~

Today is Thursday. Guess what happened? Mrs. Richards, the cheerleading coach, my Physical Education teacher asked me to run a four-forty yard for a grade. While I was running, I was thinking about Willie and Patricia and the shadow man. I beat everyone, I won! Coach Richards suggested that I ask my parents if I could try out for track and field. Guess what else, Momma said yes.

~ ~

Today is Friday. A few of the boys that live in the neighborhood asked if they could grind on me with my clothes on. I let them; I don't know why. They pushed me against the side of my house outside in the back and they did it.

~ ~

Today is Saturday. I have been busy on the track team, doing my classwork and my chores at home. I am doing well on the track team but not so good with my class work and I got suspended for fighting again. Yesterday I had another fight with a boy on the school bus. His name is Pork Chop; I don't know why people call him that.

He told me that he was going to beat me up at the bus stop so all of his friends got off to watch him beat me up. He was waiting for me on the bottom step of the bus. I jumped from the top step on top of him and beat him up. His friends pulled me off of him. That was my third bus suspension. I was certain that Momma was going to be mad with me.

~ ~

The boys picked on all of the girls, but especially me. One day on the bus, LaSalle kept talking about my daddy walking down the street with crap in his pants. I got up from my seat and confronted him. As I stood over him, I slapped him in the mouth and we started fighting. The bus driver pulled the bus over to pull LaSalle off of me. I was suspended off the bus for two days.

~ ~

Today is Sunday. It has been eight months and one year since I wrote to you. It has been a long time and I am still running track. I run cross country and nothing is more important to me than running and winning. When I am running, I feel wanted. I feel that I belong to something and people like me. I am a sprinter. My coach calls me Wilma Rudolph; that makes me happy. All of my friends are on the track team; Vivian, Gail, Paula and Beverly. Gail, Beverly, and I are on the four by four mile relay. I love the one hundred ten Hurdles. We won the All County eight eighty medley relay and I hold the county title for the one hundred ten hurdles. Raymond and

Clarence are my number one fans. They are always at my track meets, even when we went to the Florida relays in Gainesville. They were always waiting at the finish line. When I ran they yelled, "Lean, lean into it." I didn't want to lose a race and see them disappointed, so I vowed to win every race and did.

My coach entered me in the women's pentathlon. It was my first time participating in an event like that. There were five events: hurdles, high jump, long jump and eight eighty. I was afraid of heights, so the high jump became challenging for me. I found it hard to relax, jump the bar and fall back onto the mat. I jumped as high as I could. When it reached five feet ten inches, I panicked and would stop and go under the bar onto the mat.

The one hundred ten hurdles, my favorite race was coming up. I was assigned to lane three. My coach said that my time was the best, and I could win the race if I stay focused. I saw everyone looking at me stretch. As I was waiting for the starting gun, I focused my mind to win. The race started and out the blocks, I was sprinting and cleared the first hurdle. I was focused, remembering my form and I cleared the next four hurdles. Suddenly, it happened; my steps were off. At the fifth hurdle, I lost my count and my lead leg tipped the hurdle. I went sliding underneath the sixth hurdle. I was totally devastated. I got up, brushed my bruised knees off and started running to jump the remaining hurdles. Of course I finished last, but I got a standing ovation. Everyone stood to applaud me, even my competitors. Running track and cross-country was something that needed me and I needed it.

Vivian, Valencia and Juanita surprised me for my birthday. I met them at Juanita's because her mother was out of town at a church convention. When I got there, my boyfriend Chief, Vivian's boyfriend Al, and Juanita's boyfriend Mike were there. Valencia's boyfriend wasn't there; she left after we ate to be with him. We had chicken cacciatore. We had so much fun. I love my friends and Chief.

~~~

Today is Tuesday. Today is the first day of school. I am glad I worked over the summer, so that I could buy my school clothes. I am running cross country and track again this year.

~~~

Today is Monday. Thanksgiving is in a few weeks. Guess what happened to me? Last Friday after school, my Uncle Raymond's girlfriend Nikki, took me to get a perm. When the lady rinsed the perm out of my hair, all of my hair went down the drain. I was bald! Nikki and the stylist kept saying, "It's a good thing you have a keen pretty face."

I went home and cried. I would not come out of the house for a week. When I went back to school, some laughed at me and called me names. On the school bus coming home, LaSalle said "Hey, look at bald headed Kim with her black ugly ass. Wait until we pass by her broke down house that looks like an old lady shack. I saw her daddy walking down the street with wet sagging pants with do-do in them – Do-Do man and Bald Girl."

When I saw the bus driver laughing, I got up from my seat. I heard the bus driver say "no walking while I'm driving."

"Shut up," I said. I got in LaSalle's face and hit him in his eye and we started fighting. I could hear everyone saying, "it's a fight…it's a fight!"

LaSalle pushed me off of him and jumped on me and hit me in my head over and over until the bus driver pulled him off of me. I don't know what will happen to me after high school. I still hate my life, Willie, Patricia, Nikki and LaSalle. I broke up with Chief.

~~~

Today is Monday. This may be my last time writing. Willie got married; his wife's name is Angela. She has three children: Anisa, Jonathan and Jaron. They moved to Highland, Texas. Finally, he is out of my life.

Grad night was fun. We saw Kool and the Gang; we had a lot of fun. Vivian, Gail, Karla and Paula have plans to either join the military or go to college.

Last Saturday, Momma went gambling in hopes of winning some money for us. While she was away, Coach Rudolph called. He asked to speak with Momma but I told him that she was not here. Coach Rudolph told me that I qualified for a track scholarship. He was confident I had time to take the required college testing before training began. I was so excited, then something happened – fear overshadowed me. I was scared. I began to think who would be here for my Momma if I go to college? I don't know how to live without Momma. What if I don't score high enough? What if I can't run as fast as the coach think I can? My mind was flooded with "What Ifs." Needless to say, I did not pass the message to Momma to call Coach Rudolph. For that matter, I didn't share the phone conversation with anyone. When anyone asked if I heard from any recruiters, I said, "No."

Dear Dairy, this is the end.

Chapter 5

Willie Guess What?

Strawberry Cake

Going to pick strawberries with family and friends to later sprinkle sugar over them or to create a mixture to put on top of the cake was something I looked forward to. I took my boys to the "Strawberry Festival" every year. This cake is my son's favorite cake; as a matter of fact, strawberry flavor is his and mine favorite ice cream.

I graduated from high school with no plans. I had no idea what to do with my life now that I had messed up a chance to go to college on a Track scholarship. Why didn't my family prepare me for life after high school?

While walking from the Lil' General Store getting Sonia, Momma and Daddy cigarettes and loose tobacco, I ran into Kelvin and his sister. Kelvin graduated three years earlier. I knew his family. His brother and I attended the same school.

Kelvin asked me to go riding with him in his new black Pontiac Firebird. I was surprised he asked, but I felt comfortable enough to say yes. When he came to pick me up, he got out of the car and came inside to speak to my parents. The evening went fine, and we had a good time together. When he dropped me off, he walked me to the door and asked me to be his girlfriend. The next day he took me to meet his mother and sisters. Afterwards, we went to the beach, a drive-in movie, and dancing at the Sugar Shack.

Things were going really good with Kelvin and, for a moment, I didn't think about the missed scholarship opportunity. As things were kicking into gear with Kelvin, Willie phoned. He called to tell Momma that he wanted me to come live with him and Angela in Texas. He offered to enroll me into college. He added that he spoke to the coach and that I can tryout as a "walk-on" for track and field or cross-country tryouts; I need to make a decision quickly. Momma gave me the message, but she also added that I will be back if I decide to move because I will not like living with Willie. I heard what Momma said, but the chance to go to college was too tempting, so I decided to leave for Texas. With my excitement, there was also a weird feeling in my gut that Momma was right and that things would not work out. I ignored the warning because I really wanted to run track.

I called Kelvin to let him know that I had an opportunity to move forward with my college career and run track. He wasn't happy with me leaving and went so far as to say that he will move to Texas in a year to be with me. I didn't say anything about his offer to move to Texas. I heard what he said, but the only thing that was on my mind was running track again. After we said our good-byes, I got the feeling that my move would be the end of our relationship.

Highland, Texas here I come! I did not waste any time in getting to Texas. I moved in with Willie and Angela, and on the surface everything appeared fine. Within a few weeks, Willie and Angela had their first argument in front of me. Angela was strong; she stood up to Willie when he went on his drunken escapades.

One day, they were arguing about who was going to cook dinner, and Angela told him to go take a bath because he was getting on her nerves. Willie gave her a look of revenge at her tone towards him. He went into the bathroom and about five minutes later he yelled "Angela come here." "What do you want, Willie?" She yelled back. "Come here and put your ear to the door; I want to tell you something." Angela put her ear to the door to hear what he had to say, and, with abrupt force; he pushed the door open, hitting her in the head. He was as they say "38-Hot" at Angela for yelling at him; he got his revenge. I started yelling at Willie, asking, "Why would you do that? She is bleeding, you big dummy." A few days after this incident, Willie and Angela were back to normal whatever that was.

I ran five miles daily so that I would be ready for tryouts. Oddly, I found myself tired constantly and having trouble staying awake during the day. For some strange reason, I wanted to sleep all the time. One evening, Willie was cooking dinner that consisted of fried chicken, pig feet, rice, collard greens, and cornbread. Dinner was almost finished when he noticed that he needed more beer. He asked Angela to watch the food while he went to the store.

I was in my room taking a nap when I was awakened by a foul smell coming from the kitchen. I stormed into the kitchen asking, "What is that you are cooking?" Before Angela could answer, I started to throw up so I ran to the bathroom. While in the bathroom, I heard Willie coming through the front door. As he entered the house, "Willie guess what?" Angela said. "What?" he answered. "Kim threw up," she said. "Kim is pregnant, Willie." She told him to forget about putting me through college. Willie was angry and said, "I know she did not bring her behind down here with a baby." I went back into my room and placed towels at the bottom of the door to prevent the smell of flesh from seeping into my room. Willie knocked on the door, but I did not answer. He yelled through the door, "Are you pregnant?" I said, "No, it is the scent of those pig feet cooking that is making me sick."

Two days later, Willie and Angela told me that they were taking me to the track tryouts at the college. As we were on our way to the college, Willie made an unexpected right turn into an office park. He slowly pulled up to the front of an office building with a sign that read "Medical Office." I did not know what was happening so I said, "I thought you were taking me to the track tryouts at the college." They both ignored my question. When Willie parked the car, I was told that I needed to see a doctor.

When the nurse called my name to see the doctor, Angela went with me into the examination room. I was afraid because I had never had a doctor examine me "down there" before. Angela showed no compassion but simply said, "Well, there is a first time for everything; you will be fine." When my test results were ready, the doctor called me, Willie and Angela into his office. Immediately he said, "Kim is pregnant." I responded with "Kim who?" He repeated himself looking at Willie, and Angela. "I am not pregnant," I said. "You been having sex, haven't you?" Willie asked. I don't remember what happened next. When I came to myself, I was back in the car heading home. "Do you think you are smarter than me?" Willie asked. "You left Tampa pregnant thinking I would take care of you and your bastard baby. Yeah, you think you are slick but I got something for you as soon as we get home."

When we arrived at home, I felt something wet in my panties, so I went into the bathroom. I stood over the commode, dripping blood. I had blood in my panties and in the toilet. I yelled, "Angela, I don't know what to do." "Do about what?" she asked as she entered the bathroom. I moved away from the toilet and pointed. "Willie, we have a problem. Kim is losing the baby." "Where does it hurt, Kim?" Angela asked? Angela told me to shower and change into clean clothes. Willie phoned Sonia to tell her that I was pregnant and that I had come to stay with him so that he could take care of me and my baby. He told her that I will be leaving his house tomorrow and returning to Tampa. He also told her that I did not want to go to college which was not true, so I yelled, "That is not true! I want to go to college, and, even now, I still want to go."

Willie hung up the phone and continued to yell at me. Angela started fussing with Willie about the way he was talking to me in front of my stepsister and brothers. Willie said, "I don't care. Send them to their room if you don't want them to hear. As a matter of fact bring your daughter Anisa out here. She needs to hear this type of mess anyway, because if she pops up pregnant, we are sending her to her daddy." Angela looked at Willie long and hard; then she said "You are a stupid man." Anisa, hearing that I have to leave and go back to Tampa, she started to cry, begging me not to leave.

The next morning, Willie and Angela took me to the airport with all my things and a pack of cheese crackers. When I arrived in Tampa, I told Sonia about the blood, so she took me to the doctor to make sure I was all right. Unfortunately, there was nothing the doctor could do. My baby had died a few days before. I lost the baby…I lost my baby…I lost my baby! I named her on the airplane ride back to Tampa. Her name was Monique Love Daye.

I called Kelvin to let him know that I was back in Tampa and inform him about the tryouts and the miscarriage. A few weeks later, I met Kelvin when he got off from work at City Park to talk about our relationship. As we sat in his car, I begin to explain to him why I wanted to break up with him. He felt that we could work things out, but I insisted that we break-up.

Baking Through My Brokenness

    Kelvin was upset about the breakup and, with no warning, took a can of mace and began spraying it in my face. I opened the car door and ran to my cousin's house which was across the street from the park. I banged and kicked on the door, screaming for Yolanda to open the door. When she opened the door, I was wiping the liquid from my face. She asked, "Who did this to you?" "My boyfriend, Kelvin," I replied. She walked me to the bathroom and ran water over my face until I could see clearly.

    I told Yolanda that my boyfriend sprayed me with Mace because I broke up with him. As we sat in the living room talking, we heard a loud crash outside. We ran to the window to see what was happening. People in the neighborhood ran outside to see what made the loud crash sound. When Yolanda and I ran outside, we saw Kelvin's black Pontiac Firebird smashed into the concrete column in the park's pavilion.

    He crashed his car because the fumes from the mace got into his eyes, causing him to lose control of the car. After seeing that Kelvin was fine, I went back into the apartment to call his mother and let her know that Kelvin was in a car accident.

    That was the End of Kim and Kelvin!

Chapter 6

Not Again

Caramel Cake

This is a delicious, moist, brown sugar cake. I fell in love with this caramel cake; he was 10 years my senior with the perfect caramel complexion and a full beard. Baking this cake reminds me of my first heartbreak when he asked me to do something that I totally disagreed with. The only good and sweet experience that came from this relationship was my first-born son. He is my sweet slice of caramel cake.

Reflecting back to my experience last summer with Willie, I promised myself that I would never speak to him again. If you want to know the truth…I hate him. To be honest, I have hated Willie since my Momma and Daddy told me that Willie was my dad and not my brother.

Speaking of Willie, I was baffled to learn that he asked my brother Shelton to come live with him in Texas. As Shelton drove away, Momma and I said simultaneously, "He'll be back." We laughed so hard that we cried.

I desperately needed a job, and that was no laughing matter. To my surprise, my sister-in law came through for me. She recommended me for a file clerk position with the school board. It was a temp position but it did not matter; I needed a job so I took it.

On my way to work, I often stopped at the Café' Con Leche and Cuban toast at the Tropicana restaurant. One morning while sitting at the bar waiting for my order, I saw a tall brown-skinned, handsome man with a full beard walk in. In a deep raspy voice he said, "Good morning. I see you every Thursday morning when you pass by the shoe shine stand, walking into the Education building. I would like to take this opportunity to say, "You are a very beautiful young lady." I said, "Thank you." As I was walking away, he said, "My name is Harry Johnston, and I would like to take you to lunch or dinner." "My name is Kim," I replied. He pulled out a business card and flipped it between his fingers to write down his telephone number. I put his card in my purse and left the restaurant.

My heart was racing with excitement. A day or so later, I phoned him and we decided to see each other. He was an older, more settled man, unlike the young men I dated. I knew that I was in over my head. I was 19 years old, pretending to be an adult, dating a man ten years my senior, but I did it anyway. I couldn't tell Momma that I was involved with an older man; I was forbidden to associate with any man older than I was.

Harry was divorced with four children: two boys and two girls. He introduced me to his mother, sisters and brothers. It was his routine to drop me at home after work and then return a few hours later and take me dancing. I spent my weekends at Harry's, and on Sundays he would take me back home. One day when Harry drove up to my house to drop me off, Momma was sitting on the porch. She motioned for Harry to get out of the car. Nervously, Harry walked towards the house. He introduced himself to Momma as Harry Johnston, the man who is in love with your daughter. Daddy shook his hand and invited him to stay for dinner but Momma was concerned about his age and asked him to tell her the important things she needs to know about him. Harry shared a lot about his personal life; after two hours of talking, laughing, and some frowns, Momma said "OK, I approve of your relationship with my daughter."

As I became more involved with Harry, I discovered that I was not in love with him. I realized that I was impressed with dating an older man but I was not in love with the older man, I was dating. Around the same time that I was wrestling with my feelings about Harry, he confessed that he had lied to me about his marital status: he was not divorced. He told me that he wanted to marry me, but he had to wait until his divorce was final. This revelation did not bother me because I was not in love with him.

Shortly after he told me that he was still married, I missed my monthly cycle. When I missed my cycle, I knew that I was pregnant. Another tell-tale sign that I was pregnant was the sick feeling in my stomach when I came in contact with the smell of certain foods.

I had to let Harry know about the pregnancy the next day when he was driving me home from work. I told him that I was pregnant. He blurted out, "Get an abortion. I have an eight-month old child, and you need to abort that baby." As I stepped out of the car, I yelled, "That's stupid!" I slammed the car door so hard that the window shattered, and the glass splattered to the pavement.

As I entered the house, Momma was frantically preparing a home remedy for daddy who was sick with a fever, vomiting, and a headache. "Call Sonia and Clarence, tell them we need to take your Daddy to the hospital," she ordered.

On the way to the hospital, I rehearsed my conversation with Harry in my head. I could not believe his response to my pregnancy. Daddy was admitted to the hospital; he was very sick. The next day, I went to the doctor to confirm my pregnancy. The doctor told me that I was five weeks pregnant. At the same time that I was learning that I was pregnant, my job with the board of education ended. I vowed to support myself and take care of my child so I got a job at the Burger Connection.

Days later, Daddy passed away in the hospital from complications of liver and lung cancer. Standing at the gravesite in all black, I felt empty and full of life at the same time. I needed to tell Momma that I was pregnant, but I was embarrassed. Being pregnant by a man who wants me to abort my child is not happy news. To avoid the look of disappointment in her face, I decided to leave my prenatal vitamins on top of the television. When I returned home from work, Sonia's car was in the driveway. As I walked in the door, Sonia blurted, "Is this how you tell Momma that you are pregnant?" I told her that I didn't know how to tell her, so I took the easy way out. By the way, I broke up with Harry because he asked me to abort the baby.

Shortly after Daddy died, Momma became sick. I lived in a constant state of fear and depression because Momma was ill. I could not feel my heart anymore because I was filled with sadness. When I looked into the mirror, I no longer saw my happy face. The woman that played a huge role in saving my life was sick. My family tried to keep her illness from me, but I knew she did not feel well because I saw her drinking raw eggs, Ensure, and coughing up mucus. When Sonia took Momma to the hospital, she was diagnosed with walking pneumonia. I watched hopelessly as a healthy, vibrant woman turned into a frail, weak woman.

As I was leaving the hospital, the nurse pulled me aside to tell me that Momma was scheduled for surgery the next morning and would be in recovery all day. I knew I had to ask God to heal Momma:

> Dear God,
>
> I know that I have been sad and dark, but Momma is really sick and I am scared. I heard someone say that she misses Daddy. They were young when they got married, and now he is with you. Momma was admitted to the hospital last night. Please heal her so that she can see her great-grand child. God, please. I need her to be home with me when I come from the hospital. I need her to teach me how to be a good mother.
>
> God, last night when I was there, I told her that I have been praying for her to come home. She laughed at how big my stomach had gotten. She touched my stomach and said a prayer for my baby. I missed her at home laughing at me getting bigger; I can't see my feet anymore.
>
> Thank you, God.
> Kim Elizabeth

The day after surgery was the last time I saw Momma. She was in a lot of pain, but she smiled a little when I held her hand. After my visit, she developed complications from the surgery and passed away.

When I was told that Momma had passed, I became numb. I was pregnant and lost. How can I be someone's mother when I just lost the person whom I needed to teach me how to be a good mother?

I was adamant about attending the funeral because I didn't get the chance to say goodbye. I didn't get the chance to kiss her. I asked my girlfriend's mother, Ms. Rice, was a Registered Nurse and an excellent seamstress, to make me a dress to wear to the funeral, and she agreed.

Following the wake, there was a large amount of tension in the family. Willie demanded that I give him the money Momma had given to me for my baby and me. When I refused, he said that I placed too much stress on Momma and that is why she is dead.

The funeral service was scheduled to begin at 3:00 pm the next day. Late morning, I walked out of my room and told Sonia that the baby was coming. She took me to the hospital, and after the first examination they said I was fine. At the second examination, the nurse broke my water. Needless to say, I missed the funeral. Missing the funeral caused me tremendous stress which hampered my labor and delivery. I could not dilate beyond five centimeters so the doctor elected to perform a C-Section.

I remember getting prepped for surgery but nothing else. When I woke up in recovery, my girlfriend's mother, Ms. Rice, was standing over me, holding my hand, making sure I was OK. She made sure I knew my baby was fine and noted that she was filling in for my family.

The next day from my hospital room, I called Harry and his mother to tell them that I have a beautiful baby boy. Harry's mother came to the hospital to see me and brought her grandson a gift. Both of my friends' mothers came to see me. Harry never came to the hospital to acknowledge his son. I left several messages asking him to come to the hospital to sign the birth certificate, but he never showed up or called me back.

My best friend, Vivian, called from Korea to suggest a first name for the baby. I named my son Du'Ron Henry. I vowed that my son would have a relationship with his grandmother. I committed to take him to see her once a month.

The first day home with my baby was lonely; I had no parents. My aunts came over with money and cases of milk. I didn't need pampers because I purchased about 20 boxes in different sizes over the course of my pregnancy. My sister, Yvette, dropped by to bring baby items that my nephew had outgrown. As we were sitting and talking, Yvette told me that she was sorry that my Momma (Josephine) and Daddy (Henry) were gone, but they were in a much better place with God.

Then out of the blue she said, "I have something to tell you." I shook my head motioning her to continue. She went on to say, "Kim, this is not your blood family. This is Willie's family, and he is not your real father. Your real father lives in Orlando, Florida."

I didn't understand why she was telling me this. I was sitting on the sofa with my baby in my arms listening to Yvette and then I stopped listening and only wished that she would leave. I did not want to hear this horrible news. It was déjà vu all over again. It suddenly darned on me that I was sitting in the same spot on the sofa when I was told that Willie and Patricia were my parents. According to Yvette, my Momma and Daddy were not my grandparents, Willie is not my daddy, and my real family lives in Orlando. I asked Yvette to leave, I wanted to be alone. She gave me a long stare, then she hugged me tight before leaving.

I felt angry, disappointed, abandoned, rejected, unimportant, lonely and unloved. I could not go through another wave of deception again, so I rejected everything Yvette said and I avoided discussing it with her further. I decided that I didn't care what my sister said. Willie is my daddy; my sister must be confused.

The following week Patricia and her husband Ruben stopped by to see me and my baby, her third grandchild. I wasn't overly excited to see Patricia; we simply did not care for each other. She walked into the house with several bags of baby clothes. I expressed my gratitude to her and Ruben with hugs and kisses.

While Ruben walked outside to grab more bags from the car, I began sharing with Patricia what Yvette told me about my daddy. Before I could tell her the whole story, she told me to stop talking. Her husband didn't know about her family dynamics and she did not want him to know. She told me that we would talk about it later.

How do you prepare a young immature woman who has just lost her parental grandparents for the news that they were not her blood grandparents? At any rate, I did not want to deal with it even though eventually I would have to deal with it. I was turning 21 in a few months and I only wanted to focus on my baby and beginning a new life without my parents, whom I will always love and miss dearly.

The following year, my family went to Winter Garden, Florida with my maternal grandmother to visit family. My cousins and I walked across the street to the Juke-Joint. There was a handfull of people standing around the pool tables and a few people at the bar. As we were walking out, the bartender pointed at me and said, "Wait a minute. I know your Momma, Patricia Mae." What he said next was mind boggling: "Kim, I am your daddy." I looked at him and kept walking. When I told Patricia about it, she said, "He is not your daddy. I know who your daddy is; I was there. Your daddy's name is Wallace. As a matter of fact I don't want to talk about Wallace or Willie anymore…The End."

I finally dissolved what was left of my relationship with Harry. We could not agree on co-parenting, and he refused to pay child support. I told him that he could never reach out to my son or me. In spite of my non-existent relationship with my son's father, I continued to take Du'Ron to visit his grandmother. I was determined that my son was going to have a relationship with her.

Chapter 7

Catch Me Please

Sock-It-To-Me Cake

I was a broken and desperate 22 year-old young woman who could relate to this delicious cake title. No one invites physical abuse into their lives. I am blessed that God put someone in place to catch me.

I had something to prove to my mother, Patricia. Unlike her decision to give me away, I wanted to show her that I could raise my child by myself. I didn't need or want to give my son to a family member. My mother had five children, and she did not raise any of us from birth to adulthood. I was determined to be a different mother than she was.

I wanted to be loved and have a man to share my life. I was single, young, and very naive with a baby when I met Derrick. Shortly after we met, I invited him over for dinner, and he never left, until he was forced to. He took over my lovely, low-income apartment, me, and my 18 month old baby's life. Derrick had deep, piercing, soulless eyes which prompted mystery and also alarm bells which I ignored.

After a few weeks of living together, Derrick asked me to get a baby sitter for Saturday night because he was taking me somewhere special. I was excited to do a date night. I assumed that we would go dancing and drink a few rum and cokes. I wore my favorite blue dress with the back out and my favorite gold sandals. On our way to my special surprise, we dropped Du'Ron off at my maternal grandmother's house. With no baby for the evening, I couldn't wait to get the evening started.

Derrick drove for a while and then he stopped the car in front of what appeared to be an abandoned house. "Why are we stopping here?" I asked. Derrick got out of the car and walked around to the passenger side. When he opened my door, I was reluctant to get out. He reached for my hand and snatched me out of the car. Walking up to the side door of the house, he forced me to hold his hand. When we went inside the house, I was shocked at what I saw: it was a crack house. I could not believe what Derrick was getting me involved in. He never let go of my hand. He led me to a man-made table top that was nailed to the wall. He released my hand and said, "Do not move and I mean it." He walked over to a room; when he returned, he had all the necessary paraphernalia needed to smoke crack cocaine.

He said, "Relax, it won't hurt, and I will not let anyone bother you." Somewhere in my soul – the Holy Spirit begin to intercede for me because only God could save me at that point. "Watch me, and you can do it next" he said. I felt tears running down my face. I was just about to scream when he looked into my eyes. I could see death in his eyes, and his face seemed to channel a demonic force. I watched and my soul prayed. When it was my turn, I said, "No, I want to go home." I took one step backwards but Derrick grabbed my wrist and said, "Get your ass back here and enjoy this with me before I slap you." I inhaled once or as they say "I hit it" once and then I said, "I want to leave now." He said, OK. Just let me hit this one more time and then we can leave.

When we got into the car, the Holy Spirit was still interceding for me because nothing happened to me from smoking the cocaine. The drug had no effect on me whatsoever. I felt nothing, absolutely nothing.

This incident made me realize that I had made a bad judgment call getting into this relationship, and it was time to put an exit strategy in place. I knew that I had to get my son away from this crazy man.

A few weeks later, Derrick and I were sitting on the sofa watching a movie and my son was across from us asleep on the loveseat. There was a knock at the door, and Derrick looked at me as if I knew who it was at the door. He looked through the peephole and said, "It's a dude." When he opened the door, it was my ex-boyfriend from high school. I invited Wesley in. I introduced Wesley to my boyfriend Derrick. Wesley started to apologize for intruding and not calling before stopping by. His visit was short and he shook Derrick's hand and apologized again for intruding as he left. Wesley and I had dated a little after high school, and since that time we remained good friends. I stopped by his parents' house to say hello a few months ago. There was a spark when I saw him recently, but we remained friends.

After Wesley left, we continued watching the movie as if we had not been interrupted. After the movie, we grabbed a bite to eat, and then I got ready for bed. I kissed Du'Ron good night and put him to bed.

Hours later, I woke up to an excruciating pain. It was worse than going to the dentist or delivering a baby. While I was asleep, Derrick repositioned me to my back, placed his knees on my forearms, and put his butt on my chest. He then began to wake me by hitting me in the face over and over again.

When I opened my eyes, there was pure darkness, then I saw small glimmers of light and stars from the force of his hands to my face. As he hit me, he accused me of cheating on him and disrespecting him by having my lover come to his house. When he felt the need to stop hitting me, he said, "Don't ever disrespect me again." I apologized and pleaded with him to stop hitting me. Finally, he stopped and I was able to get out of bed, take a bath and get dressed for work.

When I was ready to leave for work, Derrick insisted that he drive me to work. I asked if we could take my son with us, but he said, "No, he's sleeping next door, and why would you want to wake him up? Are you stupid?" I wanted to run but not without my son. On the way to work, I told Derrick that my supervisor was not going to let me work because my face was badly bruised. He then said, "Go inside and tell her you were in a car accident and come right back out…you have 10 minutes."

As I entered the building, I remembered that my supervisor was the RN on duty for the night. I thought perhaps when I told her that I was in a car accident, she would exam me and call the police while Derrick was still outside. When I walked into her office, she looked at me and asked, "What happened?" She tried to touch my face, but the wave of her hand towards my face caused me to jump. Then she said, "Who hurt you?" I stood frozen. I could not say anything. She told me that I could not work because my face was bruised and distorted. She told me to go home, take a few days off, and call her when I was feeling better. As I was walking back to the car, I knew that things were going to get worse before they got better.

Six weeks later, Derrick and I had an argument. We were arguing because I was next door visiting my neighbor when he arrived home. I went next door to pay the neighbor for babysitting. While Derrick and I were going back and forth about the length of time I was at the neighbor's home, Du'Ron was sitting quietly on his tricycle watching his favorite television show.

Without warning, Derrick hit me, and I fell to the floor. As I fell, I could see Du'Ron in front of the television in a trance watching his favorite show. I reached for the gun underneath the bed, but I couldn't grab it. The room went dark. "Kim, can you hear me?" Aunt Lillie came by the house and found me lying outside on the ground. She tried shaking me to wake me up, but I did not respond. When I regained consciousness, I screamed, "Where is my baby? Is he OK?" Aunt Lille told me that my son was fine and she had called 911. When the ambulance arrived, she took Du'Ron home with her.

On the way to the hospital, the medical technician told me that my boyfriend and I were fighting and he had thrown me out of the window. A man was standing outside, and looked up when he heard scuffling, and saw you tumbling through the air. He tried to catch you but missed; however, he was successful in breaking your fall." He then said, "You are a lucky young lady."

I spent the night in the hospital for observation. While lying there lifeless from the emotional and physical pain, I thanked God for saving my life. It was the Lord who caused a man to walk out of his apartment and sit on the air conditioning unit, three stories below, just as my body came tumbling towards the ground. The man was able to brake my fall. Oh my, hell must be upset because, again, the Lord delivered me out of the devil's hands.

I was released the next day from the hospital, and my uncle Clarence and Willie took me back to the apartment. The window screen was underneath the bed with strands of my hair attached to it. Apparently,

Derrick tried to push me through the screen but when that failed he pulled the screen off the window and threw me out.

One night, shortly after I escaped Derrick's attempt to kill me, I was outside walking towards a friend's apartment. Derrick came up behind me, grabbed my arm and tried to force me into his car. He said he wanted five minutes of my time to talk. When I refused, he picked me up and covered my mouth so that no one could hear me scream. As he was trying to put me into the car from the driver's side, I managed to get out a scream or two. I was struggling to release myself from his grip when he bit me on my back. I screamed, clinched backwards, and he bit me on my thigh. Then, out of the darkness, a large massive shadow standing about 7 feet tall came running towards the car like "Andre the Giant." Derrick must have seen him coming because he reached into the car and pushed me out onto the ground and sped off. The gentle giant pulled me up off the ground and then walked away. A neighbor called the police and when they arrived, I provided a full description of the attacker.

Back at my apartment, I was packing Du'Ron's clothes when Derrick walked into the room. I didn't hear him come in. I was sure I had locked the door. He said, "Don't be scared. I promise I'm not going to hurt you; I just want my family back. Let's go to my Momma's house, she has been asking about you." I couldn't breathe, I couldn't think. My heart stopped pumping, I was frozen in time.

I got in the car with him and we left. We pulled up to a check cashing store and he asked me to cash a check for him. As I examined the check, I noticed that it was a Social Security check. Immediately I said, "I am not cashing this check." He hit me in the mouth and was going to hit me again, but someone walked out of the store and saw him so he stopped. We left the store and headed to his mother's house. When we pulled up to the house, he said, "I'm pissed at you, so let me go in and get a plate of food for us and I will be right back. I'm taking the keys." Waiting for him in the car, I realized that the ignition was broken and the car would start without the key. I jumped over to the driver's seat, pressed the pedal to the floor and took off, almost hitting a State Trooper as I drove away. I kept thinking, why didn't that trooper pull me over?

I arrived at Sonia's house and felt that I was safe at the moment. Later that night, Derrick set my apartment on fire; I lost everything I owned. My son and I eventually moved in with Aunt Sonia. I quit my job and enrolled in night school. One night, Willie dropped me off at school; I was almost 10 minutes late. As I walked to class, I saw Derrick moving quickly down the hall towards me. I began running towards the administration office. I ran past the secretary as she yelled, "Hey you can't…." I ran into the Dean's office and attempted to run behind the Dean's chair so that he and his chair could protect me. Derrick reached for me with his left hand and motioned to stab me with his right hand but the Dean intervened. Instead of stabbing me, Derrick stabbed the Dean and then ran out of the school. After this incident, I spent my days in paranoia; I was afraid to leave the house. I had an appointment with the District Attorney, but out of fear, I canceled the appointment. I knew within my gut that Derrick was following me.

At night, I held Du'Ron close to me. I made sure to keep him in my arms, full of love. I rocked both of us to sleep each night, singing, "Come by Here, My Lord." I needed God to protect my baby, my family, and my friends from Derrick. I went to sleep each night, singing, and praying that God heard me calling for his protection.

One morning, I was reading the newspaper and the headline read, "Woman Stabbed to Death." It happened in the apartment complex where Derrick's mother lived. As I read the article, I recognized the name; it was the young lady who lived in the building next to his mother's, and I remembered her. She was very nice and friendly. She and Derrick's mother would talk often. I was so troubled that I didn't leave the house for weeks. I was also too afraid to sit on the porch for fresh air.

One day the phone rang, and when I answered, it was Derrick. When I heard his voice I froze - it felt as if he was standing behind me. He asked if I would meet him so that he could apologize. I hung up the phone and cried, and I did not waver from asking God for protection.

A few weeks had passed since Derrick phoned, and I felt that I had enough strength to walk to the local convenient store. As I turned the corner towards the store, I observed two police officers in an unmarked car. I stepped into the phone booth to call the District Attorney's office to ask if these officers were looking for me. I could not reach the District Attorney assigned to my case. As I was leaving the phone booth, one of the officers asked if I was Kim, and I said, "Yes." I asked to see their badges and if I could call someone to let them know I was with two police officers at the convenient store. I called my aunt and explained what was happening and told her that I would call her later.

The police officer told me that they stopped me to talk about Derrick. They asked, "Have you been watching the news or reading the newspaper? That young lady who was killed a few weeks ago, we know who killed her; he left his fingerprints behind. We know where to find him, and we also know about all the attempts on your life." As the officers were driving me home, they told me that I would be subpoenaed to testify during the trial.

The following Sunday, there was an article in the newspaper announcing that the killer of the stabbed victim had been captured and was in custody. God heard me…Amen! Derrick was sentenced to life in prison.

Kim Elizabeth Russell

Chapter 8

Mr. & Mrs. Did Others
Red Velvet Cake

There are several occasions celebrated when deep dark red roses are given as a symbol of love. The Red Velvet Cake shares the same platform. This is the dessert that takes center stage on the cake table. It can be partnered with several cake flavors. For me and my bleeding heart, this cake reminds me when love, commitment and a vow became just crumbs on a plate.

The way I met Aaron was somewhat of a hook-up. Allison and I were getting ready for lunch when she decided to write her name and number on pieces of paper and hand them out to men. Her plan was to approach potential men, strike up a conversation, and give them her number. If they engaged in a conversation with her, it was a sign that they were interested in her. Allison was ready to replace her baby daddy. She knew that she was "hot," pretty, and prepared. Allison tried to get me to join in with her plan but I wasn't feeling it. Maybe I could meet my husband by joining her plan but I didn't want to do it. The truth…I was as desperate as Allison was to get a man, but I didn't want to admit it.

As Allison and I were walking through the parking lot into the mall, she gasped, "There he is dang yummy yum good. He is fine, Kim, watch this." Allison purposely put herself in his path to make contact. When their eyes locked, she said, "Hello, my name is Allison. You are a good looking man, are you married? Will you take my number and call me sometime?" I waited a few steps away, thinking to myself that she is too bold; I would not have the courage to approach a man and give him my number. He was handsome: brown complexion, about 6 feet, 180 lbs. and rocking a full beard. She walked away from him switching with thumbs up and a big smile on her face.

After returning to the office, I told one of my co-workers about the "handsome guy" we met in the parking lot. As I started describing him, my phone started ringing and I had to answer the call. When I answered the phone, the caller said "Hello, Kim, how are you?" "I am well, thank you for asking, how are you sir?" "My name is Aaron; I met your co-worker Allison earlier today." "OK, hold for a moment, I will transfer you to her." He abruptly said, "I called to talk to you. I saw you before Allison approached me." He went on to say, "I was actually on my way to introduce myself to you when she jumped in my path. By the way, I just spoke to Allison and explained to her that I am not interested in her, but I am very interested in you so she transferred me to you." Now that you know the real, how do you feel about that?" he asked. "I am flattered," I said. "Flattered enough to give me your phone number?" he asked. I gave Aaron my phone number and after the first phone call, he never stopped calling.

Aaron told me that he was divorced with four children: two boys and two girls. It did not take long for us to fall hard for each other. I accepted his children and their Momma because I loved him and he told me that he loved me. Before falling asleep each night, Aaron always said, "I love you, Kim Elizabeth."

Aaron shared an apartment with a roommate named Steve. When I visited Aaron, Steve would almost never be there. Aaron often said, "Steve is at his girlfriend's house." One evening while visiting Aaron, he told me that he had a surprise for me. He said that he locked in on my subtle hints about the summer concert and that he was going to take me to the concert. I was so elated that we were going to the concert that I said, "That is why I love you, Aaron Russell." He told me that Steve and his girlfriend were also going to the concert, and they would meet us there.

On the day of the concert, Grandma Annie agreed to keep Du'Ron. As I was getting ready for the concert, it dawned on me that I had not heard from Aaron all day. I phoned him earlier in the day, but he did not answer the phone. I became concerned because the concert was starting soon and Aaron was cutting it close by picking me up so late. I didn't want to miss the opening comedy act before the concert so I drove to his apartment. When I knocked on his door, no one answered so I began knocking harder. My knocks were apparently loud because the next door neighbor opened her door to see what was wrong. When Aaron did not answer the door, I drove back to my place thinking that I may have missed him and believed that he would be at my apartment waiting for me.

"Where are you, Aaron?" I screamed as I pulled up to my apartment with no sign of his car. By now, it was too late to go to the concert so I decided to get undressed, avoiding the mirror so that I didn't have to see the disappointment in my face. I went to bed that night and cried myself to sleep. After a few hours of sleep, I decided to get dressed and drive back to Aaron's place. When I arrived, I did not see Aaron or Steve's car. Driving back home, I thought that perhaps he had been in an accident or maybe something had happened to Steve and Aaron was with him as I wiped the stream of tears from my face.

Tomorrow came, and it resulted in another day of not hearing from Aaron. I went to his apartment, and this time Steve answered the door. I pushed the door open asking, "Where is Aaron? Where have the two of you been and why is no one answering the phone?" I opened the door to Aaron's bedroom shouting louder, "Where is Aaron? Is he OK?" Steve said, "Kim, he is not here. You have been running your tail over here every day; yesterday you came twice." "How do you know I came by yesterday and what kind of games are the two of you playing," I said. In case Aaron was hiding in the house, I yelled, "If you don't want me, be a man and say it to my face."

Steve motioned for me to sit down. As I calmed down, Steve said, "The next-door neighbor is my step-brother, and he told me you came to the house yesterday and today. I told Aaron not to leave without telling you he wouldn't be here any longer. I thought the four of us were going to a concert. What are you talking about before he left? Did he move back to Georgia?" I asked.

Steve said that Aaron had never bought the concert tickets and that now he was out of town with his ex-girlfriend, Monica. My heart started to beat faster. I couldn't identify where the pain in my body was coming from. It was either coming from my heart or my stomach. Tears were beginning to swell in my eyes. Steve saw the look on my face and said, "Kim, you can do better than Aaron. He is still messing around with Monica. I shouldn't be telling you his business; I am violating the man code. I think you are a good girl, and I believe you should know because there is something special about you. Actually, you remind me of my sister." He stood up and reached for my hand to walk me out the door.

I headed back home but I couldn't let Du'Ron see me upset so I needed to get it together before I picked him up from his Grandma's house. I tried to put on a happy face when I arrived at Grandma's house but when she saw me; she knew that something was wrong. She always knew when something was bothering any of us. "You should have a backup Kim," she said. "Huh," I said. "You heard me, you should always have a backup," she said, looking directly into my eyes.

Months after this incident, Aaron called constantly, but I refused to answer his calls because I wanted him to feel what I felt. One evening I decided to pick up the phone and talk with him. In a harsh tone I asked, "What do you want, Aaron?" "Can I come over to explain?" he asked. "Kim, I promised her before I met you that I would help her drive her kids to their grandparents in Thomasville, GA, for the summer. Furthermore, my wife asked me to give the marriage another try, and I said yes. She and the kids will be here tomorrow." I replied, "I don't want you any more Aaron. I met someone else and he is on his way over here. Your things are by the door."

Several months passed before I saw Aaron again. One morning, there was a knock at the door and it was Aaron. When I saw him, there was happiness in my eyes. He said, "Kim, I made a huge mistake, I don't love my wife anymore, and I want you. I am going to ask her to sign the divorce papers again."

"I don't know why I love you or why I put up with your mess Aaron. When I met you, you told me that you were a happy, divorced man." "Do you think she will sign the papers this time?" I asked. "I am going to make her sign the papers," he said. "I will call you in a few days; she should be gone soon." A few days passed and I did not hear from Aaron. I thought it was a sign that he was taking care of business.

In the midst of the Aaron drama, I missed my period. I went to the drugstore to pick up a pregnancy test. I was in shock as I stared at the "positive" indicator on the stick. My cousin Kay was in town for a visit and staying with me. When I saw the positive pregnancy test I screamed, "Kay, I am pregnant!" I immediately wanted to find Aaron and tell him the news. Kay rode with me to Aaron's place. When we arrived at his place, there was a U-Haul parked outside. I was so excited and thought that Aaron's wife was really leaving this time. When Aaron got back together with his wife, she moved into his apartment that he shared with his roommate Steve. When I saw the U-Haul parked outside, I decided that I would wait to tell Aaron that I was pregnant.

As we were leaving, I saw Steve walking towards his apartment and stopped to say hello. Before I could say anything, Steve blurted out, "Aaron is not here, he is at Monica's place. His wife has been staying at the apartment but Aaron has not been around. His wife is leaving him today. You can find him with his girlfriend, Monica. "Steve, what are you saying? What are you talking about?" I asked.

Kay accelerated the car before Steve could respond. "Take me to the apartments on the corner of Fletcher and Washington," I demanded. "How do you know where that chick lives?" Kay asked. "I remembered he told me where she lived months ago," I said. Kay pulled into the parking lot of Monica's apartment complex. I got out of the car, walked up the stairs, and knocked on the door. The door opened, "Yes, can we help you?" said two young boys. "Tell Aaron to come to the door," I said. "Ma, there is a lady looking for Aaron" one of the boys yelled. "Why are you at my front door? Aaron is not here," she said. "Tell Aaron that I am pregnant and we need to talk," I said. "You black cow, get away from my house with that bastard baby," she demanded. I didn't bother asking her to repeat what she said. I slapped her in the mouth, grabbed her by her hair, and pulled her out of the doorway of her apartment and beat her yellow behind. "Kim, stop it!" yelled Kay as she pressed down on the horn. Monica's sons were yelling, "Stop hitting my mother!" I went down the stairs and she got up and started chanting, "Black cow and bastard baby." Kay drove me back to my place.

On the ride home, I started berating myself for believing that Aaron had changed. Here I was pregnant again without a husband. I was disappointed that I allowed Aaron to come back into my life. I don't understand why I allowed Aaron's baggage to invade my happy, single life.

It wasn't long before Aaron showed up at my home. Apparently Monica had told him about our fight at her home. Aaron begged me to open the door so that we could talk, and I did. I told him that I would not tolerate cheating or disrespect if we continued with our relationship. Aaron promised that he would change.

My second baby boy was born on Mother's Day. Aaron was excited to have another son.

One day Aaron took the boys to get a haircut. I told Aaron that I would have laundry and cleaning completed by the time he got back and we could catch a movie. I turned up the volume on the music while I was cleaning because I was feeling great. The ringing of the phone interrupted my music jam. When I answered the phone, a woman said, "May I speak with Aaron." I couldn't believe that a woman was calling my house asking to speak with Aaron. "Who is calling?" I asked. She replied, "Look you black cow, if you don't put Aaron on the phone, I will come to your house." I said, "No problem, I will be outside waiting for you."

A few minutes later, a car sped around the corner and parked next to my car. I walked out of my apartment down the sidewalk with my gun to meet the woman. As I was pulling the gun from behind my back, I pressed it firmly in her face. The woman replied, "Hold on, what's going on? It's not me you want, I'm Keisha. I am here to visit my girlfriend." The woman points to an apartment across the hall from mine. Lowering the gun and moving aside, she walked passed me, down the sidewalk, and knocked on the door of the apartment directly across from mine. The door opened and she entered the apartment.

After weeks of arguing with Aaron about the phone call, he finally admitted that the neighbor across the hall had introduced him to Keisha one day while I was at work.

A year later, Aaron ask me to marry him. I asked Patricia if she and her husband would cater the reception. She said, "No, we will not if you marry Aaron. Have you forgotten about all the heartache he has caused you?" Have you forgotten about that night when your brother Anthony told you that he saw Aaron's car in the projects every weekend over at some woman's house that has six children?" She continued to say, "I do not like him, your brothers do not like him and your sister is not coming to your wedding because you didn't make it to her wedding." Although Patricia did not like Aaron, I felt that she owed me one. I am her daughter. Paying for the reception would be a great way for her to make up for some of the heartache and pain she has caused in my life.

When Aaron came home, my conversation with Patricia was still on my mind. As we were preparing dinner, Aaron said, "Kim, we will be married in three weeks, are you ready?" I asked, "Do you have your divorce papers?" "Yes, they came yesterday." It was a relief to know that the divorce was final and maybe this was a good sign.

The wedding day finally came. During the ceremony, when the pastor was ministering to both families, I started to cry. It wasn't because my birth mother wasn't there or the fact that the woman that raised me wasn't there to kiss my cheeks. My tears came from a place of desperation and love. Aaron had disrespected me a thousand times over and now I was standing before God and these people committing my life to this man. What if he does it again? What will I do?

It was the end of summer and everything was going good for me and Aaron. I was home alone because Aaron, Du'Ron and Dre were gone to Savannah. I was on the phone catching up with a girlfriend who missed the wedding. She missed the wedding because her mother was sick. As she was apologizing, I received a call waiting click and I told her to hold on while I answered the incoming call. When I said hello, a deep voice demanded to speak to Aaron. I told the caller that he was is in the shower because I was at home alone and didn't want the caller to know it.

"Is this his wife," he asked? "Yes, I am his wife," I said. "I have something to tell you about your husband" he said. My heart skipped beats, but you would think by now, I should have been familiar with this type of call. Anything that involves Aaron and his mess should not surprise me. We had been married six months and I could only say, "Here we go again."

While I was waiting to hear what Aaron had done, I heard someone in the background yell, "Hang up the phone." The man replied, "Shut up, I'm talking to his wife. I told you that I am calling all of the numbers in your secret phone book." The man then turned his attention back to me. He told me that my husband was having an affair with his wife. The female in the background demanded that he give back her phone book and hang the phone up. They started to argue, and then the phone went silent so I hung up the phone.

I couldn't believe this was happening again. I cried myself to sleep and vowed that I would ask Aaron for a divorce. When Aaron came home, we put the boys to bed, and I told Aaron that we needed to talk. I told him about the phone call and told him that I wanted a divorce. He told me that the person who called was lying and he was not going to give me a divorce or an annulment.

A month later, Aaron's car broke down, and I had to drive him to work at 2:00 am. I woke Dre up to take him with us. When we got back home, I put Dre in his bed and then I went to bed. I was drifting off to sleep when I felt a heaviness climb in the bed and position itself next to me. I was under the covers, and "the presence" was on top of the covers. When I realized that it was not Dre, I began to pray and call on the name of Jesus. As I said, "Jesus," the presence lifted off the bed and left the room.

Someone had told me some time ago that I needed to stop allowing these different spirits (men) into my home. I was told that these spirits hang out in the corners of your bedroom, bathroom, kitchen, living room, or all over your house. I never forgot this and that is why I started calling on Jesus.

Aaron began pursuing his dream as an owner operator truck driver. He enrolled in a truck driver course that required him to be away from home for six weeks. I asked Aaron if we could talk about our marital issues before he left for his training course, but he wanted to wait until he returned. While he was gone, I had plenty of time to think about our marriage. As I thought about all of the wacky things that had gone down in our marriage, I realized that I was a fool for love. Our primary focus was our six children. When we talked, we only talked about the bills and the kids.

When Aaron returned from his training course, he seemed different. He was attentive to me and my needs; however I wasn't vested in the marriage anymore. Truthfully, Aaron never stopped cheating on me and subsequently, I started cheating too.

My cheating started when I got a job as a secretary at the church where I was a member. One of the Pastor's friends came by the church at least three times to go to lunch with the Pastor. Before long, I found myself attracted to my Pastor's friend.

The phone calls from Aaron's women, his late night antics, and the daily fighting and arguing made it easy to drift my attention away from Aaron to another man. Ivan dropped by to see the Pastor three times a week. I was attracted to Ivan and I believed he was attracted to me.

One day the pastor was in a meeting, and he asked me to let him know when Ivan arrived. When I saw Ivan coming through the door, I stood up from my desk to go tell pastor that Ivan was here. Before I walked away, Ivan said that he was not here to see the pastor today. Instead, he told me that he was here to see me. Then he asked, "Are you happily married?" "No," I said. Are you going to leave him?" he asked. "One day," I said. Ivan started making advances towards me, and I did not reject them.

Ivan and I started hanging out. With all the cheating Aaron was doing, his cheating didn't affect me anymore. I was happy with my relationship with Ivan. My boys spent some Saturdays at Ivan's sons' football games. Afterwards, we went to his place to cook dinner or order pizza. The relationship lasted for a long time. I don't know if my marital situation became old to Ivan or if it was time for us to end our relationship.

One Sunday during Worship Service, one of the associate pastor's walked over to me and said, "Sister Kim, you walk around with a cool demeanor denoting that everything is good, but I can see your pain." The pastor overheard the conversation, and he begins to pray for me. I began praying inwardly. I was disappointed in myself that I had to reach beyond my marriage for attention and love and was very upset that I allowed myself to become involved in adultery.

When pastor finished praying for me, he said, "Sister Kim, you spoke in your spiritual language."

In addition to my marital problems, I became angry about the things I was exposed to at the church. The things I witnessed caused my countenance to fall, and, before long, I had fallen into a dark place battling rejection.

The following school year, one of Du'Ron's high school classmates committed suicide. It affected me and my sons very deeply because we knew him very well; we considered him family. He was a loving, talented, intelligent, handsome, young man, and he will forever be missed. RIP our "shining star".

I found the courage to leave Aaron. My sons and I moved in with Willie and my step-mom. One evening, I received a phone call from my cousin "T". She heard that I had left Aaron and was back in town. After catching up, she told me that she had something to tell me. This is what she told me: One Saturday, I took my son to the barber shop for a haircut and met a barber from Largo, Florida. He was in Tampa spending the weekend with a cousin. He told me that he would give my son a free haircut if I gave him my number. After my son's haircut, the barber, who was staying in the same apartment complex as me, rode with me back to his place. As we went through the security gate, your sons saw me and ran up to the car to say hello to my son. I asked where you were and they said you were at the nail salon next door.

The barber asked, "How do you know those boys?" I told him that they are my cousin's boys. Then he said, "Kim is your cousin?" "Yes, and why are you asking?" He said that he had been trying to hook up with you since the first day he saw you but you would not give him the time of day with your fine, sexy self. I told him that you were married and off the market. He then said that your husband spends almost every night with his cousin therefore, you don't have to be faithful to him.

After hearing that my husband has been unfaithful for months or maybe longer, I was embarrassed. I told my cousin that I've heard enough, and I hung up the phone.

I could feel anger swelling in my soul. I decided to change clothes and confront the woman who was having an affair with my husband that my cousin "T" told me about. I wasn't sure of the exact apartment, but I knew that she drove a Green Beretta so I drove around the apartment complex looking for her car thinking I would most likely figure out which apartment is hers. Just as I was about to turn around and go home, I saw her taking groceries out of the car. She didn't see me so I waited for the right moment before getting out of my car.

When she took the last bag of groceries into her home, I went up the stairs a few steps behind her. She left her door open, so I reached in and knocked on the door then politely stepped back out of the threshold. "Who is it?" she yelled. "I am looking for your cousin that cuts hair," I said. "He is not here this weekend: leave me your name and number, and I will tell him to call you. I will bring you something to write with, she said."

As she turned towards me unfolding a piece of paper, she looked up and immediately froze. We stared at one another for a few seconds, and then she muttered, "Kim, I am sorry. I was wrong to date your husband, I am sorry." "Say it again," I demanded. It was a delight to see the fear on her face and hear it in her voice. She was trembling and frozen at the same time. I stepped up to her face. We were breath to breath and nose to nose. Unsure of what I would do next, she took a step backwards but I was not about to back down so I took a step forward so that I could stay in her face.

Unexpectedly, I slapped her; she was shocked. I hit her hard because I wanted to leave my handprint on her face. She grabbed her face, and I shouted, "Yes, you are sorry. You are a pathetic, pitiful woman. You are a nasty Cow, that's what you get for sleeping with my husband, upstairs above me. You need to know that I left him so you can have him. She said, "He doesn't want me any more." I told her that he never wanted her silly ass because he will always love me. I politely backed out of her doorway, walked down the stairs, and got into my car and drove off.

I called Aaron and he answered, "Hello Wife." I said, "I know about the woman you messed around with who lived above us." He immediately said, "I did not mess with that woman, Kim." I told him to sign the divorce papers and I hung up.

It was Saturday night, and I was getting ready to go out on the town when Willie said, "Kim, you are in the streets too much. You need to stay home with your children." "Daddy, please stay out of my business; the boys are going to bed."

As I was ironing my boy's uniforms before I left for the evening, I heard the word "whore" slip from Willie's mouth. "What did you say?" I asked.

"What are you talking about?" he said. "I heard you say, I am carrying on like a whore," I said. "Well, are you Kim?" I thought about all the women this man has been with, and he has the nerve to call me a whore! The devil kept putting ugly thoughts in my mind. The devil told me to confront his ass and, better yet, go get the gun and ask him to repeat it again.

Willie went into the kitchen and sat down. I approached him (without the gun) and said, "You called me a whore. A Daddy should never call his daughter anything other than a princess. "No!" he yelled. I told him to look at me but he would not look at me. I said, "The women you cheat with are whores; you are confused." I then got in his face and placed my index finger in the center of his forehead and said, "As long as you live, never call me a whore again or I will bury you next to your Daddy. That topic never came up again.

Chapter 9

You Better Not Hit My Mother
Devil's Food Cheesecake

Lord forgive me. I made a mistake when I shared my sheets, panties, and emotions with the Devil. I exposed my son and my niece to the abuse I accepted. The only thoughts I had when I realized what I had gotten myself into were to believe that God will provide the exit plan.

I was committed to my New Year's resolution, "Never lose sight of what I knew was right and remain in alignment with the word of God."

One day after dropping my son Dre off at the barber shop to get a haircut, I decided to treat myself to breakfast at a very popular restaurant in downtown Atlanta which my best friend Trina talks about all the time.

I had not been downtown since the Jill Scott concert last year. Standing in line to pay for parking at the electronic meter, I saw a distinctive, good looking man three or four people ahead of me. He kept looking backwards as if he was waiting on someone. When I got inside of the restaurant, there was a wait for a table. After about 22 minutes of waiting, I could not wait to get a table. I ordered coffee with cream, a mimosa and the #2 with a side of grits.

"There is a good-looking couple," I thought to myself as they walked by my table and then I recognized the man; he was the man who kept looking backwards while I was waiting to pay for parking. He was a very good looking-man, and she was rocking some bad-looking shoes and on- point with an Italian leather bag.

Waiting for my check to pay for breakfast, I got a phone call from my girlfriend Trina. She wanted to go to the outlet mall to pick out our birthday gifts. I told her that I needed to run an errand and would pick her up in about 20 minutes.

A new boutique on 8th Ave. was having its Grand Opening so we decided to go there. I found a cute outfit and went into the dressing room to try it on. As I was walking out of the dressing room to get Trina's opinion of the outfit, I noticed the chick from the restaurant who was rocking those bad shoes. A few seconds later, I saw the man who had been with the lady with the bad shoes. I thought that this was really beginning to feel weird. Apparently, I was staring at the man too hard because Trina asked me who or what was I looking at. I told her that I would explain later.

While I was in line to pay for my purchase, the man came up next to me and said, "My name is David. This must be fate because this is the third time I have seen you today." I said, "I disagree that fate has anything to do with it." "Where is your girlfriend?" I asked. "She is not my woman; she is my step-sister" he said. I can introduce you to her if you want." I told him that it was not necessary, it was nice to meet him, and have a great day as I walked away. He yelled, "Wait, what is your name, please take my number, and call me later, I would like to show you this is fate," he said.

On the way to drop Trina off, she told me that the man deserved a phone call. I told her that I am not feeling him at the moment. For some reason, I didn't believe the woman with him was his step-sister and even if she was, I am doing something different at this juncture in my life. As Trina was leaving the car, she said that he could be "the one," so give him a call.

I was headed to pick up my son Dre when I got a call from Trina. She told me that she snatched the phone number from David's hand after I refused to take it. She left the piece of paper with his phone number on it in the passenger side of the door.

I couldn't believe she grabbed his number. Well, maybe Trina is right; I decided to give him a call. I called him, and we talked the entire 45 minute drive to pick up my son. He lives in Texas and owns a small landscaping business. All I could think about was my sexual abstinence vow and my "no more sheets" escapades.

Months have passed since meeting David, and, of course, I broke my abstinence vow. I just threw my sheets in the laundry with an extra cap of Clorox.

The following year David asked me if I would consider moving to Texas. He told me to remember the word "fate" as I pondered my decision. Every day, I got either a good morning phone call or a good night phone call. I waited until David was in town to give him the good news that I was able to transfer my job and I could move this summer to Texas.

"How does Dre feel about moving?" he asked. "Dre is happy as long as he is with me," I said. "I will find us a house to lease" he said. Willie called while I was out celebrating my move to Texas with Trina. Willie told me that Clarence is very sick and he may not make it. He told me that I needed to get here as soon as possible. Later that night, I shared the sad news about my brother's illness with David. While we were talking, he purchased airline tickets for me and my sons and said that he will meet me in Tampa.

Dre and I had a good visit with Clarence. When I left, I knew that it would be the last time I saw him. Clarence was my big brother who didn't judge any of my stupid mistakes. He was encouraging, supportive, and I love him and I know that he loves me and my boys.

It wasn't long after the visit, that I got the call from Willie that Clarence passed away. I was devastated. Losing Clarence was a different type of heartbreak. I felt myself losing sight of the light when Clarence passed.

Trina drove Dre and me to the airport. When we arrived at the departure gate, David was there waiting for us. "I was not going to let you go through this by yourself," he said as he hugged us.

At the funeral service, I was reading the funeral program and it said that "He leaves to cherish his memory a loving wife of 32 years, 4 daughters, 4 sons, 2 sisters, and 3 brothers. "I said, wait…I am listed as a sister, not a niece." I felt the presence of love and respect hugging me, and I cried in David's arms. His parents raised me as one of their children and he considered me his sister; I knew he loved me. I was surrounded by my family, my loved ones, and my girlfriends at the funeral. The pain of not having my favorite uncle any more hurt. He was always there for me when I needed him, he always gave the best advice and he meant everything to me.

The last night in Tampa, Willie invited everyone over for dinner. He and I had the most loving conversation we have ever had. I was telling him about my new job and the move to Texas. "Kim, be very careful with David. A man is different in his own city. He seems like a good man for you and Dre in our presence, but he may change once he gets you and Dre away from us."

Instead of flying home, we decided to drive back to give my uncle Leroy a ride home to South Georgia. The ride back was an eye opener. David's true colors were coming out; a sneak preview of what was to come. He was the worst back seat driver. He kept telling me which lane to drive in, how fast to drive, where and when to stop for gas, even the conversation with my uncle was controlled. When we reached Leroy's place, he called me inside for a minute and said, "Kim, you need to be careful with that man. I know his kind, and he is not right for you or Dre."

When we arrived to my apartment, we were exhausted and I was still grieving from the death of my brother. Before falling asleep, David insisted on talking about the trip and how I did not listen to him. "Are you the man in this relationship, Kim?" he asked. "I am firm but fair and what I say is what will happen; don't cross me again," he said.

At our new home in Texas, Dre was excited about his new school and the basketball team. David found us a nice home with 4 bedrooms, 3 baths, 2 car garage, wood-burning fire place, hardwood floors, and a spacious back yard. When he opened the garage door, there was a new Chrysler 300 parked. "This is for you," he said. "Honey, I told you that I am loving, firm, but fair. The only things we need for the house are new appliances to replace the outdated ones. One of my clients had a moving sale and I bought a refrigerator and a gas grill. I have been calling the client all day to schedule a time to pick up the appliances. I put cold hard cash in her hand, and she is not answering the phone."

David was noticeably getting angry. I was about to suggest that he remain calm but before I could, he placed his forefinger on my lips while shaking his head. He said that he did not ask for my two-cents and that he's got this. "Wow," I said. "Say another word and that smile will be upside down" he said.

A few days later, we were driving home from meeting his parents and some of his friends and their wives when David said he still had not been able to reach the lady that he bought the appliances from. I said, "Let it go, we will save our money to purchase them brand new." There was dead silence; you could only hear the engine running. I think that the music playing even went silent out of fear of what's to come.

We made it home without incident. I was getting undressed standing in front of the mirror, thinking I may need to work out because I am getting fat, David grabbed my arm with force and twisted my arm behind my back and said, "If you ever offer your unsolicited advice again, the next time it will be worse. One of two things will happen: I will get my money back or we will get the refrigerator I paid for."

The next day, to make up for the comments and my unsolicited advice, I purchased the appliances we needed for our new home. When David came home from work and saw the new refrigerator he said, "So you are the provider, huh?" So you are the man with the stick between her legs, huh?" I was trying to explain why I bought the refrigerator but then everything went blank. As I was getting up from the floor, I started to cry hysterically. David begin to kiss away my tears. "If you would just think before you speak and really shut the hell up, I wouldn't be kissing your tears, we would be planning for our future or did you forget we have a wedding to plan," he said. When I looked into his eyes, I realized that he was just stringing me along, and we were never going to be a married. I swore I saw a two-faced coin.

The following day, I was pulling into the driveway and David pulled in behind me, blowing the horn. He yelled, "Get out the car." My son and I got out of the car. He told Dre to go in the house and do his homework because I and your mom need to run an errand.

David wanted me to go with him to get the money from the woman he paid for the appliances. He was in a panic and I was scared. It was a 40 minute drive to an affluent, gated subdivision. David pulled up to the gate and punched the code that gave us access. After a few right and left turns, he stopped in front of a gorgeous three story brick home. There was a black Bentley coupe and a white 745li parked in the driveway. David opened his door to get out and told me to stay in the car no matter what happened. He slammed the car door and proceeded to walk up the driveway. He stopped to first look inside the Bentley and then he rang the doorbell and knocked on the door at the same time.

A woman opened the door and seemed surprised to see David. She placed her hand on her hip standing in a "WTW" position. "Where is my money?" he said. "Why are you yelling at me in my front door David?" she asked. "Who is that in your car?" she asked. "Did you bring Kim to my house David?" she asked. She attempted to walk past him towards our car when he grabbed her arm. She screamed and tried to hit him, but he had a grip on her arm that caused her to fall to the ground. He picked her up and asked, "Where is my money?" Whatever she said to him, it caused him to punch her in the stomach with brass knuckles. She folded over in pain and fell to the ground. Walking briskly towards the Bentley, he opened the door and reached for something underneath the driver's seat. The woman was still crying on the ground, holding her stomach. David got back in the car and we left. "Do not ever, ever ask me about what you saw I mean it, Kim. Do not ask me anything about what just went down," he said.

A few days after the incident, I was cooking dinner when I heard a firm knock at the door. I said, "David, please answer the door before whoever is knocking kicks it in." Dre ran to open the door instead. I heard a firm, authoritative voice ask to see David Hale. "David, the sheriff is here to see you," Dre yelled. I dropped the pan of lasagna that I was taking from the oven when I heard those words come from my son's mouth.

I ran to the door and the man said, "I am Deputy Pope and I am looking for David L. Hale." I wasn't responding, I don't think I was breathing. The Deputy said again, "Ma'am, I am looking for David Lucifer Hale, is he here?" I wasn't sure I heard him correctly, so with the perplexed expression on my face I said, "Excuse me, who are you looking for?" "Ma, he is looking for David." I will get him, Dre said.

I looked a total mess. I had on oven mitts and pasta sauce was splattered all over my shoes. I asked one more time, "Please sir, tell me who are you looking for?" I couldn't believe he was looking for the David I fell in love with – David Lucifer Hale, Jr.

I asked David in the beginning of our relationship, what the middle initial "L" stood for. He said his mother just gave him a middle initial; it meant nothing. I thought to myself, who on God's green earth would name their child Lucifer?

David walked up behind me, to answer to the sheriff, "I am David L. Hale" he said. David was arrested for domestic violence and violation of probation. He was taken into custody from our home, in front of my son. According to the attorney his mother hired, the court date will be in six weeks. I never asked David why he hit the woman nor did I ask about what he took out of her car.

During the time David was incarcerated, I rented a storage unit large enough for household items I could not take to Florida. I also left my child support checks in the storage unit to keep safe if for some reason David was released before I had time to execute my plan to leave Texas.

Baking Through My Brokenness

As David's attorney was getting ready for the trial, I learned that David was involved with the woman with the Bentley; it was her twin sister who sold him the appliances. He told me that he was involved with her before meeting me but it wasn't anything serious. He said she was in a position to invest in his landscaping business and other business ventures. He told her that he was going to marry me; she told her sister and that is why she kept his money. He claims that he paid her for the appliances because he didn't want any problems after I got here but she wouldn't let it go.

Forty-eight days later, David was released. He came home wanting to proceed with plans to get married. That night, David got dressed to leave home and I asked, "Where are you going?" "None of your business, but if you must know to my Mother's" he said. "Who are you, the county detective?" he asked. "If you think that you are going to question me I will stay at my parents tonight," he said. When David walked out of the door, my chances of leaving just got better. If I could somehow manipulate him to stay "with his parents," I could leave before morning.

The next morning while Dre was getting ready for school, David returned home. He entered the bedroom with a devilish smirk on his face. "Good morning David, are you hungry?" I said. "No, Kim, my Momma cooked before she left for work," he said. "Did you sleep well?" I asked. "Why are you asking me all these questions?" he asked? "What are you talking about? This is what couples that are in love and planning to get married ask," I said.

I went to take a shower. I turned around to rinse my back off and saw David looking down at me over the shower door. I screamed and he just looked at me. I was so upset, I didn't finish my shower. I turned the water off and grabbed my towel to dry off. "What is wrong with you, why did you do that?" I asked. He laughed and walked out of the bathroom. I was afraid to shower when he was home and I started locking the door.

One day, with the door locked, I was taking a bath and suddenly David appeared. He jimmied the lock and came into the bathroom. He scared me so bad that I slipped in the tub. "Do not lock the door again," he said.

It became a thing for him to sneak in while I was bathing. I could not relax, I was always tense while taking a bath or shower. I had no idea paranoia would follow me like a stray cat. Dear God, what have I gotten myself into? I thought that I…And I thought you…?

One Saturday we were going school shopping. His twin boys were in the back seat, Dre was with his dad for the summer and Du'Ron was in college. I was in the passenger seat looking out the window regretting the day I met him. "I need to pack for my trip to Tampa for Mary Jane's college graduation," I said. "Baby, you cannot go to Florida to your cousin's graduation." I said, "I am a grown woman I can go and do whatever I want." He immediately made a U-turn going in the direction of home. I knew what was going to happen to me when we got home.

When the car came to a complete stop at the traffic light, I told myself to *get out of the car, run, and go now Kim!* Suddenly, I jumped out of the car, running through traffic, dodging cars trying to get into the convenience store for protection. I ran through the store looking for a safe place to hide and made it into the women's restroom. He must have been right behind me because seconds later the metal bathroom door was pulled from the metal hinges and I was pulled out of my hiding place. I was snatched out of the store, in front of strangers and his kids. He slapped me over and over for running and when we made it home he literally kicked me in my butt.

One day Dre and I were driving home from the store. Dre asked "Ma, do you love David more than you love me?" Before I could answer, he said, "Wait I have something to add…do you love David more than you love yourself?" I was so ashamed. Tears ran from my eyes like a flood, I wasn't making any sounds. "Ma, don't cry" Dre said. "It's my soul that is crying son" was my reply. Pulling into the garage, I noticed that David was standing with his arms folded against his chest as if he was waiting for me to come home. "Not tonight, Ma, not tonight" I heard Dre's silent thoughts. I pulled in as if I did not see him blocking my path. Dre and I got out of the car, barely acknowledging David's presence. "Head nod" was Dre's response, normally David doesn't allow that. "A man speaks with his voice not his head," he said over and over.

After dinner, Dre went to his room to do his homework, and David and I watched TV. David expressed his concern that I had not responded to his advances lately. I did not want to be with him any more, but the timing wasn't right for me to make my move. David wanted me closer to him on the sofa and when he reached to pull me closer to him, I resisted. "What, you don't want me to touch you?" he said. Dre yelled from his bedroom, "I wish the two of you would stop fussing so much." David said "Shut up." "Don't talk to my son that way. I don't tell your children to shut up," I said.

David stood up and told me to shut up, and I stood up without speaking. He pushed me down on the sofa, and I asked him to stop. By this time, Dre was in the living room, yelling at David to leave me alone. David told Dre to go back into his room but he refused. Dre said, "Leave my mother alone. You have been hitting on her too long and I said leave my mother alone." David took a step towards Dre and I got up to stop him. I told him if you touch my child you will never see your children. You are on probation and I will do everything I can to make sure you never get out of jail for years. David got up, walked out of the door, and was gone for three days.

Three days later, I came home from work and David was home. He had cooked dinner, bought me flowers and made a huge sign that said I am sorry and I love you and Dre; please don't leave me. I was numb to the dinner, flowers and the sign. I pretended to have a migraine to escape the craziness.

It was time to leave David. Dre was in school doing well and begged me to try out for the basketball team. I was feeling very bad that I subjected Dre to an abusive relationship.

Within three weeks, there had been three deaths: my best friend's grandmother, who was born and died on her birthday and she also died on my birthday. The second death was Patricia's second husband, and the third death was Willie. I was emotionally affected by these deaths. Willie's passing affected me the most; our relationship was in a good place. Before his death, he told me that he loved me and I loved him. When I went to see him at the funeral home, I wanted him to get up so that we could make up for lost time.

I reminded Dre about the plan to leave Texas, but until then we could leave, I need him to remain calm. Dre understood that we needed to leave because David would not allow me to live in Texas without him. I had money saved and was able to put some essential items we would need immediately in storage.

I got a call from my District Manager at work and was told that my transfer was approved. I could not leave with my car that David bought for me, but nothing was going to get in my way of leaving, so I rented a car.

> Dear God,
> I know that I made this mess that I am in however, please make a way for Dre and I to get out of Texas unharmed.
> In Jesus name, Amen.

When David came home, he said, "I'll be back, I am going to meet a possible investor for the shop." The next morning David came home and told me that he had stayed at his mother's last night. "How is your mom?" I asked. "You don't believe me?" he asked. "If you say you were at your mother's, who am I to challenge that?" At this remark, he pushed me onto the bed, yelling, "You don't believe me?" "David, please don't start a fight this morning," I said. When I started to get up, he pushed me back on the bed and continued to ask why I don't believe him. David was interrupted when Dre knocked on the door and announced that it's time to leave for school.

I got up from the bed to take Dre to school. When I first stood up, I was afraid to move. I saw the demon in his eyes. He began pacing back and forth saying, "You don't believe me!" and I stood still not saying anything.

Then it happened; David tackled me as if I was a Royal Man Pad. He hit me with such force that I fell and hit my head on the floor; I must have been unconscious for a few minutes. I remember getting up from the floor holding my right shoulder because I was in extreme pain, and then I had a headache. I climbed up on the bed and closed my eyes for a minute or two. When I opened my eyes, David was standing over me, and I asked him, "When did you get home?" "Do you remember anything about the conversation we were having five or 10 minutes ago?" he asked. "David, what happened?" I asked.

I heard Dre yell, "I am going to be late for school if you don't hurry, Ma." I yelled back that I was coming. I could barely maneuver around the room to find my keys; I was confused. "We are coming, Dre," David said. David dressed me, we got in the car, and he drove Dre to school. "Do you have lunch money and do you have basketball practice?" Dre asked, "Why do you keep asking me the same thing, Momma?"

When we made it back home, David called my boss to let her know that I was ill and would not be in the office today. I heard him say that I had a concussion. When the morning events returned to my memory, I started screaming and crying.

The next day, when David came home, he was shocked to see the moving truck and movers loading our things. I told him if he interfered with me leaving that I would call the police. He saw the look on my face, crawled back into his car and watched all of my things get loaded into the moving truck. My move was long overdue. The time had come for Dre and me to move from this evil place David called home.

Chapter 10

There Is Nothing Sweet Here
Coconut Cake

I have always loved everything coconut. I found baking the coconut cake was therapeutic. I had to call on God's assistance again; I got myself into another flakey and raw relationship that refused to provide the sweet love of respect.

Come in, sit with me, have a slice of my Coconut Cake while I tell you how I met Mr. Right – so I thought.

My "men" decisions have only ended in heartache and heartbreak. It was time for me to figure out what my role is in picking crazy men, repent, and break out of it. So, if the Son (John 8:36) will set you free, why am I making these bad decisions?

At a high school reunion with my girlfriends Michelle and Jennifer, I met Dekaleb, a tall, dark, baldheaded, body builder.

There is no need to sugar coat this tart situation; I was desperate and lonely. Soon after meeting Dekaleb, I gave up my apartment, my furniture, and my best friend Tiger (Akita-Terrier mix) to move in with Dekaleb.

I heard it loud and clear…"Warning Kim Russell…Warning" but I ignored it because Dekaleb vowed that we would be together for 400 years. Not too much time after moving together, I became overwhelmed with an immeasurable amount of regret. One of my girlfriends had told me that it would be a good thing to move in with him. Well, it wasn't her fault that I followed her advice; after all, she had faith in his words of commitment as did I.

I needed to talk to someone about my situation and reached out to my best cousin-friend, Mary Jane. When she answered the phone, I told her that she should pour a glass of wine and I will do the same. I started the conversation by saying, "What I am about to tell you is embarrassing and I am ashamed. Here I go - I moved in with a man who is incompetent of real intimacy, tenderness, heartfelt compassion, unconditional love and warmth. This relationship is a product of my desperation to be claimed and titled. Girl, my loneliness forced me into a place of messing up…again."

At the time I made the decision, I thought it was a good one and one from God. He seemed like the man I had been praying for. I rationalized it in my head, I could not feel the light in my heart; needlessly to say, it was another bad decision.

Mary Jane has always listened and provided the best advice. There is never a situation that I needed to hide from her because she is always willing to listen. She is great with executing an exit plan if needed. After sipping on the last of the wine in our glasses, we said good night.

I woke up to the smell of a southern breakfast: grits, eggs and sausage. I was feeling good about the day. Tonight was our date night Movie and Wings. After talking to Mary Jane, I talked to God about Dekaleb. I also began to think that maybe my standards were too high. He owns his home, his car is paid for, he works full time, and he is working on becoming a fitness trainer. Also, he doesn't hang out in the clubs, he is always home. When I look at these positives, I must be tripping, I've got a good man. Oh my, I think my last name will be changing soon. It was time to get out of bed and get dressed. I put on Dekaleb's favorite shorts that he likes to watch me walk around in, sprayed a little body spray and headed downstairs to the kitchen.

When I walked into the kitchen, Dekaleb had a strange smile on his face. I knew something was up. He said that we needed to talk, and he had taken the liberty to write down a list of things he wanted to talk about but we needed to eat first.

After cleaning the kitchen, I met Dekaleb in the den. He was sitting on the sofa clinching a note pad. When I sat down beside him, he said, "Baby, I love you. Remember, me and you against the world."

He went on to say that if I agree to respect the house rules, we will be together for life. He kissed me on the forehead and gave me the note pad. On the note pad were listed the following house rules:

a) Throw out your body spray, it stinks.
b) You have too much belly fat, you could have an amazing body minus the belly fat. Your muffin top or whatever they call it is fat and it must go. I will train you in the gym downstairs.
c) Do not order wings and fries, when we go out; that's not a good look for you and stop bringing sweets and chips into the house because your body cannot afford it.
d) You cannot bake cakes, cookies or pies in this house so you should give up on your desire to become a baker.
e) I do not give flowers or cards; I haven't given anyone flowers or cards since my divorce 10 years ago, and I am not going to start now. I know you love them, but please stop mentioning flowers and stop buying them and bringing them in my house; I don't like them.
f) Do not ever leave anything in the sink clean or dirty. I do not like nastiness, and if you leave a single spoon in the sink you are nasty in my eyes. You keep the house cleaner than my ex-wife, but you need to do a better job cleaning and I am going to help you with that.
g) You have entirely too many clothes and things. Why on earth do you need so many pairs of shoes? They create clutter in my house, you should think about giving some away. When my ex-girlfriend Gloria lived here she kept her clothes neat and in one closet.
h) When you wash your car, don't leave the driveway wet, use the "Jet Dry to dry it off.
i) Stop making comments and suggestions about what I wear. If I want to wear pants with holes and covered with paint spots that is my business.

j) When my friends and their wives come over, don't invite yourself into our conversation.

After reading the list, I saw clearly he was under the influence of the devil and his dark forces. I was flabbergasted that he allowed these cruel things to pass through his lips. After reading the house rules, I thought about the state of depression and loneliness I was in when we met. Silently, I told the Lord that I was sorry that I allowed the devil to trick me, Dekaleb is not my soul mate. I began asking God to get me out of this mess I had gotten myself in.

Later that night while in bed, I was feeling stupid and thinking about Dekaleb. I felt that I deserved it for moving in with him instead of seeking God and the Holy Spirit for direction.

The shadow of rejection hovered over me while in bed with Dekaleb. I started coughing and choking and couldn't breathe. I ran out of the bedroom, down the hall into my bathroom (I wasn't allowed to use his bathroom in the master bedroom), and began to pray. I fell on my knees, crying and praying and asking for forgiveness. The crying and praying became overwhelming, and I knew that I had gone against God's will. Abruptly, the bathroom door flew open; it was Dekaleb. He asked what was wrong. Darkness surrounded him. I stopped crying but the tears kept pouring out of my heart. I imagined that the devil was sitting on his shoulder laughing. When I told him that everything was fine, he slammed the door and walked back to the bedroom. I fell to the floor crying, holding myself tightly pretending that I was in my grandmother's lap.

As time progressed, my body began to respond to the rejection and depression of needing a man. My hair was falling out by the handfull. Unbearable pain in my knees and ankles prevented me from walking up the stairs. I asked Dekaleb to carry me up the stairs to the spare bedroom I had recently moved into but he said no so I crawled up the stairs.

Soon after this incident, I left Dekaleb's place. While unpacking in my new place, I found Dekaleb's note pad with that horrible list of demands. On a different page, there was a letter he had written to me that read:

> Kim,
> I only have doubt in myself; I never had doubt in your love for me. I love you so much and I know you love me. I just want you and me to be happy in love with one another. I will put your happiness, your peace, and your love before mine. I have been thinking that it would be best for you, if I was gone out of your life. You are a beautiful woman and I feel that I am making a mistake letting you go.

Dekaleb Chambers "Big D"

I continued to unpack the things that reminded me of a broken heart, stupidity and desperation. I found one of my journals. The journal has different shades of pink with a flower in the middle; the inside is made of paper with words that only speak of loneliness and tears. If I could give this journal a title it would be "The Night Before I Died."

Dear All of My Love Ones,
I am currently treating a cold; I took cold tablets, cough syrup and four shots of the strong brown stuff and I am feeling like I want to melt away. I want to fade away in the dark. I don't want to deal with tomorrow or the next days.

Du'Ron,
You are my first love and I love you with all of my being; it may not appear that way as you read this letter, but I do love you. It was you holding my hand tight making sure I didn't let you go while walking six blocks to the bus stop to get you to head start. Be strong and always look out for your brother. I am sorry that I failed you.
Your Mother

Dre,
I can see you lying in my arms after you introduced yourself to the world. You are my second love, I love you so much. Please know that I love you. I am sorry that I failed you.
Your Mother

Eric,
The love I had for you when you were born is immeasurable. I remember the times I took you everywhere with me, you were my baby cousin; before my first born you were my first love. I love you and I am sorry.
I Love you

Sandra,
I miss Momma. Thank you for EVERYTHING, I love you

Traci,
I Love You

To everyone else,
My heart is too heavy to express the pain I am experiencing in my core. I am sorry, but I want to leave, it seems that I can't get things right and every time something goes wrong it forces me into a darker place of depression. All I ever wanted was to live, love, and be happy. Living Happy and in Love has passed me by.

Love you,
Kim Elizabeth

Chapter 11

Black Forest Cake

Turn on the Lights

What do you do, where do you hide, who can help you when you are walking in the blackest forest, where your heart has been crushed, when everyone that you have tried to love rejects you and manipulates you into separating your thighs, only to move on. The cake is architecturally made wonderful.

> "The farther back you can look, the farther forward you are likely to see."
> *Winston Churchill*

Three days ago I was convincing myself that my new year's resolution is to give up on love: "my time has passed" is what my reflection in the mirror suggested. I have written five letters to God asking him to send me my husband. Instead of waiting on God I continued to accept those who I thought were from God. The truth of the matter is I didn't want to be alone so I justified what I thought God was sending me. I have fallen in love with the man who had potential. Potentially he could love me one day, potentially he would be the man my friends and I dream about; potentially – "potentially what, Kim?" I asked myself. The faith I heard about, seemed to be a myth.

One "blue Monday" after work, driving home listening to the tires roll around on the pavement, I decided to have a "woe is me" moment. I decided to stop by the store before coming home. I pulled my aching bones out of the car, looking down, feeling depressed, and wondering what I did wrong in life to not deserve love and respect.

As I entered the store, I headed for the "Wine and Beer" aisle. As I entered the aisle, I passed a couple holding hands, discussing which bottle of champagne would go best with the dinner they were going to prepare to celebrate their first year together. Whatever, I said to myself as I looked for a bottle of wine to celebrate another year of being unloved, then I needed a bottle to celebrate loneliness, and the third bottle will be just because I ran out of the other two bottles of wine.

It didn't matter when the bottles were empty because this was a weekly ritual, shopping for my supply of wines. It became my daily regimen that I had 2, 3, and maybe 4 glasses of wine when I got home from work. Every day was a long day in my world.

When I walked in the front door of my one bedroom loft, I kicked off my four inch stilettos and walked to the kitchen to select my wine for the evening: Pinot Grigio, Pinot Noir, or Merlot. Tonight it will be Pinot Noir to pair with my bleeding heart. As I poured the deep red wine into the glass, the wells of my eyes filled up with tears and my emotions getting ready to take over. The tears begin to roll down my face. First it was just a few and then a flood of tears. I felt lonely and alone. I grabbed my wine glass and slid down to the kitchen floor sipping and crying. I cried and slurped until I cried myself to sleep. I woke up on the kitchen floor with dried tears on my face and an empty bottle of Pinot Noir. It was time to get up and do it all over again.

After work, it was time to wine shop again. I was walking down the wine aisle, not paying attention when I bumped into a tall handsome man with a distinguished smile. He started to laugh because I clearly was not paying attention. Before I could apologize for hitting him, he began to laugh. His laughter was contagious, and I started to laugh, and that is when it happened. We made eye contact for what seemed like 30 seconds. He asked my name and asked if I was married. I couldn't speak, I just lifted my left hand to show him the absence of a ring. He then asked if he could call me some time. I asked, "Why would you want to call me?" He said, "Because I see a light that shines within you and I would like to get to know you." Immediately I was impressed with his quick answer. I reached in my purse frantically looking for a pen without taking my eyes off of him. As I pulled the pin out with a receipt from last week's wine purchases, he said "My name is Jacob, Jacob A. Blackman and here is my business card with my contact information." As I reached for the card, I said my name is Kim E and proceeded to give him my number.

The relationship Jacob orchestrated for us was everything that I could ever have imagined. I didn't believe I was worthy of it. Everything about him was consistent, caring, and passionate. As time moved on, Jacob and I continued to spend time together.

During the time I was dating Jacob, I lost my biological father. I met him for the first time when I was 35 years old. It was good to meet Wallace, the man Patricia called my sperm donor. I was welcomed by his entire family. I remember the time we talked and laughed and when he hugged me and said, "Kim, I Love You, baby." The memory that will forever hold a special place in my heart is when I kissed him on his forehead after he told my two sisters and me that he was dying.

The memories of my father through the years were sketchy; however, they were mine because he loved me. I was hurt, angry, and disappointed at the same time that he was dying. I begin to question, "How did he have the unmitigated gall to die when he owed me a standing ovation at the finish line when I won the hurdle race? How could he check out without coming to my rescue when I was beaten unrecognizable? Wallace…wait before you go. Before I could continue my list of things he had missed, my father had taken his last breath.

It was my good friend Yolanda (God sent) who encouraged me to go see my father before he passed away. "Wallace is gone," I said, lying in Jacob's arms, crying; what Jacob did sent love signals down to the very core of my being. He kissed and wiped my tears away as I wept over the man I barely knew as my father.

Jacob continuously reminded me that he will never leave me and that I needed to believe in him.

> Kim,
> I am sorry about your father; he is in a better place. I want you to know that I am happy we met. I am satisfied with the chemistry of our relationship. I am not like those men from your past, just believe in me. All I ask is that you believe in me.
> Truly,
> Jacob A. Blackman AKA Your Quarterback

As clear and concise as Jacob walked into my life, he walked out in the same manner. We had gotten into a discussion and I expressed my opinion about how I thought he was responding. I think you are acting in a typical manly way, you know the "N-word" way." He said, "What did you just say?" I repeated, "I thought you were operating in a typical guy way, with an "N-word" attitude."

Needless to say, the relationship I thought we had, had an expiration date on it. Who knew that I was stamped "Use By: 03/06/2013 JB21 12:00M?"

> Who am I?
> You peeped in the window, you identified my spirit, and you pulled the door open to step into the floral shop.
> Your eyes fell on me, you pointed in my direction signaling to the shop manager that I was the one you wanted.
> You saw me blossoming into the beautiful thing that God created me to be and you desired me. You told yourself that you would take care of me.
> You promised you would adore me; all the way home, you said you would always be there for me.

Who am I?
Who do you say that I am?
Am I just a mere woman in your eyes?
But the Most High created me, there is nothing "Mere" or "Just" about me...

Who am I?
You trimmed me only once.
My stem is brown, why don't your eyes adore me any more?
Look, I am withered, weak, unfed...

Who am I?
Please, can I drink from your thoughts? I just need a little of your emotions to get me to my tomorrows.

Who am I?
I am a beautiful Flower that God Created.

That's Who I Am!

There I was, lost and broken, shopping at the supermarket where we met. Walking down the snack isle searching for my favorite potato chips; then I heard his laugh. I immediately turned around because I thought he was watching me and something about the way I walked turned him on. I turned looking for my handsome man, but he wasn't there. I know I heard his laugh, I said to myself. "Am I tripping?" I asked myself; then I heard his laugh again followed by a woman's voice.

My heart was racing and I felt as if I was going to stop breathing when I heard him say, "Your walk is um-um good to me; you go, baby, walk that walk." I walked around the aisle colliding into the woman who was receiving my compliments. The expression on our faces was, you took my man. We excused ourselves and I walked away. Jacob saw me and the look in his eyes said *nothing*, I was irrelevant. He turned around and walked out of the moment. I politely walked away as poised as I could without looking defeated. The faster I tried to walk, the heavier my legs became. Outside, I saw his vehicle leaving. I got in my car and drove off, crying all the way home.

> "A satisfied soul loathes the honeycomb, but to a hungry soul every bitter thing is sweet." *Proverbs 27:7*

The relationship with Jacob was a roller coaster ride. He made sure that my harnesses and lap bar were secure; he did not want anything to happen to me, is what he said when we agreed to get on the ride. The ride was filled with good conversation, laughter, comfort, protection and screams, then the climb to the steep hill. It was building and building, getting stronger and stronger for the great suspense and anticipation for the heart-racing emotion.

As we are sitting at the top waiting to move forward he unsnaps my harness, pulls up my lap bar and I began to slip out of the seat we both shared. I am falling, I grab onto the corner of the seat and asked him to pull me back up; he looks directly into my eyes and said, "I will let you know, just relax. I got a lot on my mind right now, I told you that I handle things differently than most, just be patient." My grip became weaker and I began to fall, still reaching for the seat, hoping that if I could only get a grip maybe he would see that I deserved his refuge, but as I slowly tumbled down I saw the devil - Lucifer himself - posted on the limb, laughing and pointing at me.

The fall was in slow motion. Unknowingly to me, it was going to be a 900 feet drop precluding to the point of no return. As I was plummeting, manipulation grabbed my hands, pulling me downward; rejection, abandonment, unloved and unwanted were on my back, riding me like a pony; physical and mental abuse and depression grabbed my ankles and then suicide, disappointment, molestation, NOT GOOD enough and inferiority, punched me in the middle of stomach.

All of a sudden, there was a heavy presence holding onto my waist, I couldn't move. It was my track scholarship that I should have pursued, my baby that I lost, weakness, insecurity - then I stopped in mid-air for a short while. I can best explain it as I was frozen in time, looking at all of the strongholds that had attached themselves to me like leeches. I wasn't spiritually strong enough to evict them.

There I was, planted in the darkest place a soul could reside, the "Manhole". When I realized I'd landed, I opened my eyes and all I saw was a mirror. When I looked into the mirror, I saw the evil spirits staring back at me. They were reaching for me to go with them. Suicide invited me to follow them and promised that everything would be OK. I started to cry and as I cried the room became darker and darker, my heart beating slower and slower as I looked into the mirror. I saw my heart turning into stone. I placed my hand on my heart and it felt like sand and gravel.

I yelled for help! I called for my Momma (Patricia). I heard her say, "Why are you calling me? Stop calling me I did not give birth to a weak daughter, get up." I called for my Daddy, but they were all dead (Henry, Willie, and Wallace). I only needed one of them.

My sisters, cousins and girlfriends were all dealing with their own life issues of happiness or unhappiness, and I did not want to invade on their lives. I was too embarrassed to call on my platonic male friend because I didn't want him to know I was weak and ashamed of judgment. I even called out to Jacob, but he had blocked my number.

No one would come to my rescue, so I began to pray and sing "Come by Here Lord." Abandonment said, "Your God is not coming by here to save you, He hears you, but He is not coming this way because this is how you are meant to live. You will never receive the love you think you should have; no one will ever love you. Your finances will never be better. So go on and continue to walk around with your head bowed down to me, (I am the prince of darkness) so that I can finish you for good." When I heard that I fell to my knees crying. Suicide grabbed my hand and muzzled my mouth, trying to pull me into a deeper place of darkness, attempting to hide me from Jesus.

"THAT'S ENOUGH" – GOD DEMANDED

I heard a voice call my name. I answered and the voice said, "If God wanted you dead, you would have died on I-75 when your car was spinning out of control, but you were unharmed. You have been manipulated into falling for someone that only wanted to play. Then she said, be blessed and have a peaceful day and trust in the Lord." I started to cry, but what about both moments when Jacob was the bird and I was the bee, the well of his eyes filled with water and "I believed he was into me."

The next voice said, "Kim, you are a strong powerhouse. The devil has been trying to kill you since birth. You have work to do, there is someone that needs to hear your story, get up and walk with God. He is there waiting for you, GET UP!"

There was a small amount of light that shined from nowhere, but it was everywhere, it filled the space I was in. The light was so bright and beautiful I had to gravitate towards it; it was calming, loving, and peaceful. The closer I got to the light, I heard loud sounds of rope popping, I felt free, released and loved.

It was God. He said, "Come, my daughter." He picked me up, placed me in the palm of his hands, and wrapped me in His blanket of Love and Grace.

God whispered in my ear, "I called you, I made you, and I have work for you to do. I love you: my Grace, Mercy and Peace will protect you. Walk on and put on the Armor of Faith and do my work. Tell a young lady your story, tell someone so that my words will heal a broken hearted soul. Now you can teach others how to stop attracting the wrong men. Tell them that Spiritual Warfare exists and the battle is mine."

The Beginning to an End…

Kimmie Kakes & Things

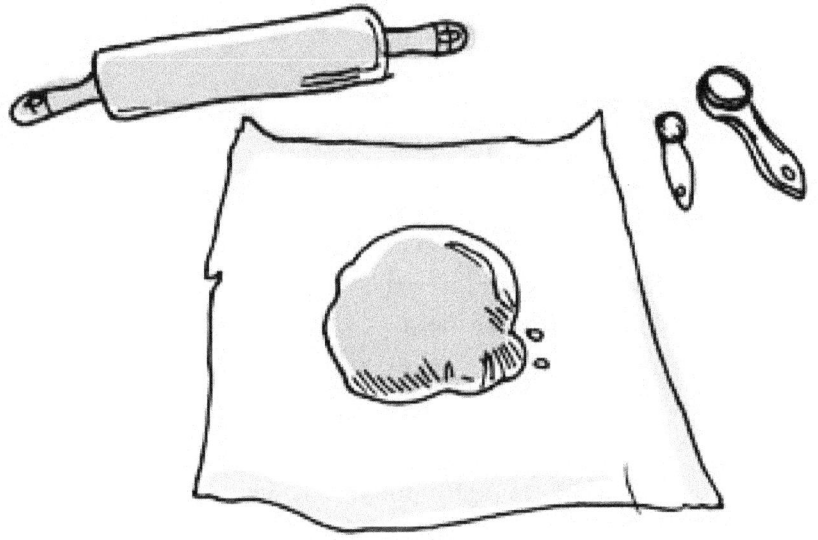

Baking Enhancers

<u>Cake Batter:</u>
- Add 1 to 2 tablespoons of meringue powder to your cake mix to help it rise a bit higher and make it a bit lighter in texture.
- Add 1 envelope of unflavored gelatin to the cake batter, helps prevent the top of the cake splitting or cracking.
- First add a teaspoon of lemon juice to the butter and sugar called for in the recipe before mixing the rest of the ingredients. Helps make the cake lighter.
- Take your time creaming the butter, beat/cream for at least 5 minutes to get lots of air into the butter. Add the sugar and beat/cream really well again.
- Separate eggs before adding them to recipes–beat yolks till golden and creamy then add to the butter/sugar mixture. Beat the egg whites until light and frothy before folding them into the butter mixture.

<u>Moister Cake Tips:</u>
- Chocolate Cake: Before adding the baking soda to your cake recipe, mix it with a teaspoon of vinegar.
- Fruit cakes/Dense cakes: Keep a pan full of water in the oven when baking the cake (replace water if needed to keep it topped up).
- Substitute oil in the recipe for unsweetened applesauce or plain yogurt. Your measure can be 1:1 or 50/50. For example, if the recipe calls for 1 cup oil, use 1/2 cup oil and 1/2 cup applesauce. Different types of cakes will offer different results for texture and taste, but a good start would try the 50/50. Not only helps for moister cakes, also cuts fat.

<u>Sifting:</u>
- Measure all ingredients to exact amounts first, then sift.

<u>Cheesecakes:</u>
- Grease the bottom and sides of the spring form pan to help prevent the filling from cracking when the cheesecake cools.
- For best results, use regular cream cheese and sour cream, unless a recipe specifically calls for reduced-fat or fa-free products

- Open the oven door as little as possible while baking the cheesecake, especially during the first 30 minutes. Drafts can cause a cheesecake to crack.

- Use a straight-edge knife to cut a cheesecake. Warm the blade in hot water, dry, slice and serve.

Custard & Cream Pies:
- Baking custard and creams pies need to be baked at a relatively low temperature to keep from curdling.

- To avoid a soggy crest when baking a custard or cream pies. The trick is to have both custard and crust hot when the pie is assembled. This allows the custard to set quickly at the low temperature.

- Refrigerate as soon as they have cooled to room temperature. Serve with a day of baking, or the crust will soften.

The Cake Pan:
- Use a paper cupcake holder, a paper towel, a piece of wax paper, the butter wrapper paper or a plastic baggy to grease the pans without messing up your hands. You could also use a pastry brush.

- Try dusting the cake pans with a bit of the dry cake mix or cocoa (for chocolate cake) instead of flour.

- Grease pan with shortening then line the pan with a piece of wax paper to fit the bottom. Re-grease the top of the wax paper. Pour in the batter. To get the wax paper to size, you can either trace the bottom of the pan and cut it out, or grease the pan, smooth a sheet of wax paper into the pan (pressing all around the creases of the pan), remove the wax paper and cut out along the crease. This is kind of a messy though, better to trace the pan then cut it out.

- To cut fat, try baking a cake without greasing the pans even if the recipe mentions to do so. You can just place a waxed paper liner to fit the bottom of the pan, then pour in the batter. This will also help remove the cake cleanly. For high cakes, you'll want to still grease and flour sides of pans if specified.

Homemade Pan Grease:
You can buy Pan Grease or make your own. This is used as a substitute to greasing the pans then dusting them with flour when directed by the recipe to

do so. Keep unused portion in an airtight container and refrigerate to use for your next batch of baking.

Recipe #1:

- Mix 1 cup shortening (like Crisco), 1/4 cup flour, 1/4 cup vegetable oil and apply to baking pans evenly with a pastry brush.

    Recipe #2:
- 2 cups of Crisco and 1 cup of flour

Baking a Level Cake:

- Fill cake pans no more than 1/2 to 2/3 full to allow for even baking and rising.

- Once you've poured the batter in the pan, wobble the pan sideways a bit so the batter reaches up along each side (with the middle being slightly lower). As the cake bakes the middle and edges will meet and rise more evenly.

- If the cake rose high and uneven in the middle when baking, you may need to slice a bit off across the top so it's level.

Oven Baking Tips:

- Preheat the oven first before starting to bake, make sure the rack is in the center of the oven (unless directed differently in the recipe) and keep pan in the center of the rack. If you're baking more than one pan at a time, keep them at least 2 inches away from the walls of the oven and from each other.

- To check for doneness, use a toothpick, wood skewer or a piece of raw spaghetti, test the cake for doneness by placing the toothpick into the middle of the cake. If it comes out clean, the cake is done.

Cake Sticking To Pan:

- Place a thick, clean towel in the kitchen sink and pour a kettle of boiling hot water over the towel to heat it (don't plug the sink to retain the water, allow it to drain out). Set the cake (still inside the pan) on the hot towel and leave it for a minute or two, the cake should turn out easily.

- Turn the cake over on a sheet of wax paper or a cooling rack. Place a clean, thin cotton towel on top of the cake pan and using a hot steam iron, heat the bottom of the pan for a few minutes. The pan should lift off cleanly.

- Cool the cakes in the pans completely before trying to remove them. Don't cool on top of the stove where there's heat, they're best cooled on a rack on top of the counter. Gently insert a knife between the outside of the cake and the inside of the pan. Run it along the pan to loosen things up before turning over.

Angel Food Cake
- When the cake has finished baking, take it directly from the oven and place it upside down on the neck of a bottle. This will help prevent the angel food cake from falling as it cools. After 30 minutes, you can turn it over then remove from pan once cooled.

Frosting & Icing
- Don't attempt to ice the cake until it's completely cool. Dust the cake lightly with a pastry brush before frosting, helps reduce crumbs in the icing.

- First ice the cake with a thin layer of frosting, then refrigerate (covered). After an hour you can do a complete frosting job. This helps keep the crumbs at bay and your outer frosting layer should be crumb free.

- After frosting the cake, you can use a hair dryer to slightly melt the frosting. This will give the frosting a smooth, glossy look. If you prefer you can use a metal icing spatula or knife first heated by sitting in hot water, wipe dry, then use the heated knife to smooth the icing.

- Have a bag of chocolate chips on hand? Just sit the whole bag in a bowl of very hot water, and mush the bag up every couple of minutes until all the chocolate has melted and there are no lumps. Snip the corner of the bag and squeeze out the melted chocolate directly onto the cake.

- Have two favorite frostings and can't decide which one to use on a layer cake? Try both! Spread one frosting on top of one layer, and spread the other on the bottom of the other layer (you'll want to flip the bottom 'up' when frosting). Then put the layers together. The middle will have a delicious two-frosting surprise :). Can also use this technique when filling the layers with a combination of fruit and whipped cream or frosting.

- To help prevent a flaking or cracking frosting, add a pinch of baking soda when mixing the frosting.

- If icing is a bit too thin or runny, lightly dust the top of the cake with flour then spread the icing on top. This will help the icing hold to the cake.

Icing Cakes:
- For one layer cakes, turn the cake upside down before icing so that the top is perfectly flat and even. When icing two cake rounds or squares, place a layer of frosting on the top of one round, then place the other round upside down on top for a perfectly flat top.

- Easily Color Shredded Coconut: Shredded coconut can be a nice, decorative touch achieved easily. Simply put the coconut in a clean jar (only one half jar full at a time), add a few drops of food coloring in your choice of color, then cap the jar and shake it until all the coconut is evenly tinted.

Cutting Cake Tips:
- Heat a knife first before cutting a cake for crumble-free slices. To heat the knife, you can run the knife under very hot water then wipe dry with a clean towel.

- Use un-waxed dental floss to slice through the cake (great for the gooey or sticky cakes).

Keep Cut Cake Fresh:
- Once you start slicing the cake, the exposed or cut sides can dry out quickly. Here's a way to keep things fresh:

- Wrap the cut cake with a few slices of fresh apple or cubes of sugar or a slice of fresh bread set inside the cake pan (or in the open space of the cake plate). Make sure to store the cake in an airtight container or wrapped well in plastic wrap.

Miscellaneous Cake Baking Tips
- Dust the cake holder or platter with a bit of confectioner's sugar before placing the freshly baked cake on it, this will help keep the cake from sticking to the bottom.

- Use ingredients that are at room temperature, the butter soft but not melted or oily.

- When mixing sticky, gooey ingredients (molasses, honey, peanut butter), try spraying the measuring cups with non-stick spray first (just lightly). The ingredients will come out easier.

- You can make your own cake flour if necessary, simply add two level tablespoons of corn starch to a one cup measuring cup, and then fill with bread flour. Sift three times then use as needed.

- Dust nuts and fruit with flour before adding to cake batter (via Fresh apple cake Recipe) or try toasting nuts first (Quick Tip: Freeze nuts). You can also just sprinkle the nuts across the top of the batter instead of mixing them in, this way the nuts will toast while the cake bakes.

- Make Bigger cakes From Mixes: To make a bigger cake from a mix, add 1/2 cup flour, 1/2 cup sugar, 1 egg, 1 tsp. baking powder.

Quick Tip: Cleaning Cake & Pie Pan Edges:
- Dip a raw potato into scouring powder to scrub the rusted corners and edges of cake and pie pans.

- You could also try using baking soda with a few drops of lemon juice.

Note: Sometimes it seems the cakes you bake just never turn out right. Try running through this list to see if you can spot what the problem may be: Why a Cake Fails. A common problem is that the oven temperature isn't true to what the dial says. Buy a thermometer, preheat your oven and test.

Cakes, Pies & Puddings

Black Forest Cake

1/2 cup milk
2 tsp plus 2 tbsp. unsalted butter, softened
8 large eggs, slightly beaten
1 cup plus 3 tbsp. sugar
1 ½ cup all- purpose flour
1/2 cup unsweetened cocoa powder
1/8 tsp salt
1 tsp baking powder
1 tsp pure vanilla extract
1 tsp chocolate imitation flavor
For the filling:
2 cups sugar
1 cup water
1 1/4 cups kirsch
2 (15-ounce) cans dark sweet pitted cherries in heavy syrup
2 tablespoons cornstarch

<u>Frosting and Garnish</u>

8 cups confectioners' sugar, sifted
1/2 cup unsweetened cocoa powder
1 stick unsalted butter, at room temperature
2 tsp pure vanilla extract
1/3 cup boiling water
1 1/2 cups heavy cream
3 tsp sugar
3 ounces semisweet chocolate, shave

Preheat the oven to 350 degrees F. In a small saucepan, warm the milk and 2 teaspoons of the butter together over medium-low heat. With an electric mixer fitted with a wire whip, beat the eggs and 1 cup of the sugar on medium-high speed in a large mixing bowl until the mixture is pale yellow, thick, and tripled in volume, about 8 minutes. With the mixer on low speed, beat in the warm milk mixture. Sift the flour, cocoa, baking powder, and salt into a small mixing bowl. Add half the flour mixture to the egg mixture and blend thoroughly until smooth. Repeat with the other half. Add the vanilla and mix gently. Grease 2 8" round pans with the remaining 2 tablespoons butter. Sprinkle evenly with the remaining 2 tablespoons sugar. Pour the cake batter into the pan, spreading it evenly. Bake until the cake springs back when touched, about 15 minutes. Cool for about 2 minutes, then gently flip it out onto a large sheet of parchment paper. Let cool completely.

For the filling: Combine the sugar and water in a small saucepan over medium heat. Bring to a boil, stirring to dissolve the sugar, and cook for 2 minutes. Remove from the heat and let cool completely. Stir in 1 cup of the kirsch and stir to mix. In another saucepan over medium heat, bring the cherries to a boil in their syrup. In a small bowl, dissolve the cornstarch in the remaining 1/4 cup kirsch and add to the cherry mixture. Whisk until it thickens, about 2 minutes. Remove from the heat and cool completely.

Assemble the cake: Using a serrated knife, carefully cut each cake horizontally in half to make 4 layers. Brush the tops of all the layers with equal amounts of the sugar syrup. (You will not need all of the syrup.) Let the liquid soak into the layers for about 30 minutes. Place the bottom layer on a large cake plate. Spread 1 cup of the filling evenly over this layer, then top with a second layer of cake. Spread 1 cup of the filling evenly over it. Repeat the same process with the third layer and another cup of the filling. Top with the fourth layer.

To Finish: Sift together the confectioners' sugar and cocoa powder into a medium size bowl. Add the butter and mix with an electric mixer until incorporated. Add 1 teaspoon of the vanilla and the boiling water and mix until smooth. Let cool. Combine the cream, the remaining 1/2 teaspoon vanilla, and the sugar in a medium-size mixing bowl and, using an electric mixer, whip until soft peaks form. Ice the sides and top of the cake evenly with the chocolate frosting. Spoon the whipped cream over the top of the cake and sprinkle with the chocolate shavings. Slice and serve the cake.

Butter Pound Cake

2 cups (4 sticks) unsalted butter, softened
2 cups sugar
5 large eggs
2 tsp pure vanilla extract
2 tsp butter imitation flavor
3 cups all-purpose flour, sifted well
½ tsp salt
½ tsp baking powder
½ tsp baking soda
1 cup buttermilk
½ cup confectioners' sugar (optional)

Preheat oven to 325 degrees F. Grease and flour tube pan. Cream butter for 5 to 7 minutes or until fluffy. Gradually add sugar, beating for 5 to 7 minutes. Add eggs, 1 at a time, beating just until yellow disappears. Gradually add sifted flour mixture alternately with buttermilk, starting and ending with flour. Mix in vanilla and butter flavor.

Pour into greased pan and bake for 1 to 1 ½ hours, until a toothpick or cake tester inserted in the center of the cake comes out clean.

Let the cake cool upside down on a greased (spray rack with any cake spray) rack.

Caramel Cake

    1 cup soften unsalted butter (2 sticks)
    2 cups sugar
    5 eggs
    3 cups sugar
    3 cups self-rising flour
    1 ¼ cup buttermilk
    1 tbsp. pure vanilla extract
    1 tbsp. caramel imitation flavor

Preheat oven to 350 degrees F. Prepare 3 9-inch cake pans

Cream butter for 5 minutes or until fluffy. Add sugar and cream for 5 to 8 more minutes. Add eggs, 1 at a time, cream and scrape sides after each addition. Add flour and buttermilk, alternately, beginning and ending with flour. Add vanilla and caramel beat well. Divide among pans and bake for 25-30 minutes until set or cake tester is clean.

Turn out of pans onto cooling racks and allow to cool completely before frosting (see cake enhancers on page # for frosting tips).

<u>Frosting</u>
    1 cup unsalted butter
    2 cups light brown sugar, firmly packed
    ¼ cup evaporated milk
    6 cups sifted confectioners' sugar
    ½ tsp vanilla extract
    ½ tsp caramel imitation flavor

Cook sugar and butter for two minutes, Stir in milk, bring to a boil and cool. Stir in confection's sugar, until thick enough to spread. Add vanilla and caramel flavor, mix lightly (do not over mix)

Spread frosting on cake.

Carrot Cake

2 tbsp. all-purpose flour
2 tsp baking soda
1 tsp baking powder
½ kosher salt
2 tsp ground cinnamon
3 large eggs
2 cups sugar
¾ cup vegetable oil
1 cup buttermilk
3 tsp pure vanilla extract
2 cups grated carrot
1 cup crushed fresh pineapple, drained
¼ golden raisins
½ cup sweetened shredded coconut
1 cup chopped pecans or walnuts

Line 3 9-inch round cake pans with parchment paper, lightly grease and flour, set aside. Sift flour, baking soda, baking powder and salt, set aside. Beat eggs and cinnamon, sugar, vegetable oil and buttermilk at medium speed with an electric mixer until smooth. Add flour mixture, beating at low speed until blended. Fold in carrots, pineapple, raisins, coconut and nuts. Pour batter into prepared cake pans.

Bake at 350 degrees for 25 to 30 minutes or until a wooden pick inserted in center comes out clean. Drizzle buttermilk glaze evenly over hot layers, and cool completely on wire racks. Spread cream cheese frosting between layers and on top and sides of cake.

<u>Buttermilk Glaze</u>
½ cup sugar
1 ½ tsp baking soda
1 ½ cup buttermilk
½ cups unsalted butter
1 tbsp. light corn syrup
1 ½ tsp pure vanilla extract

Bring first 5 ingredients to a boil in a large Dutch oven over medium-high heat. Boil, stirring often, 4 minutes, Remove from heat, and stir in vanilla.

Cream Cheese Frosting

    1 cup butter (2 sticks) unsalted, softened
    1 (8-ounce) package cream cheese, softened
    1 (3-ounce) package cream cheese, softened
    4 cups sifted confectioners' sugar
    2 tsp. pure vanilla extract

Beat butter and cream cheese at medium speed with an electric mixer until creamy. Add powdered sugar and vanilla, beat until smooth

Chocolate Pound Cake

1/4 cup unsweetened Dutch-processed cocoa powder
1/4 cup boiling hot water
1 1/2 cups cake flour
1 tsp baking powder
1/4 teaspoon salt
1 cup unsalted butter, room temperature
1 cup granulated white sugar
3 large eggs, room temperature
1 1/2 teaspoons pure vanilla extract

Preheat oven to 350 degrees and place rack in center of oven. Butter or spray with a nonstick vegetable spray, a loaf pan. Line the bottom of the pan with parchment paper.

In a bowl mix the cocoa powder into the boiling water until smooth. Let cool to room temperature.

In a separate bowl, sift the cake flour with the baking powder and salt.

In the bowl of your electric mixer, or with a hand mixer, beat the butter until softened (about 1 minute). Add the sugar and **beat** until light and fluffy (2-3 minutes). Add the eggs, one at a time, beating well after each addition. Scrape down the sides of the bowl as needed. Beat in the vanilla extract and cooled cocoa mixture. With the mixer on low add the flour mixture and mix only until combined. Scrape the batter into the prepared pan and smooth the top with an offset spatula or the back of a spoon.

Bake for about 50 to 55 minutes or until a toothpick inserted in the center comes out clean. Remove the cake from the oven and place on a wire rack to cool for about 10 minutes. Remove the cake from the pan, re-invert, and cool completely on wire rack.

Will keep, well wrapped, several days at room temperature or it can be frozen for a month or two.

Makes one loaf.

Chocolate Swirl Pound Cake

2 cups sugar
1 cup unsalted butter, softened
3 1/2 cups flour
1 cup whole milk
1 1/2 t tsp baking powder
2 ½ tsp. pure vanilla extract
1/4 tsp kosher salt
4 large eggs
½ cup unsweetened cocoa powder

Heat oven to 350°F Grease a 10" tube pan. Beat sugar and butter until blended; then increase speed to high and beat until light and fluffy.

Add flour and remaining ingredients <u>except</u> cocoa. Beat at low speed until well mixed, scraping bowl often; then increase to high and beat 4 minutes longer, scraping bowl as needed.

Scoop out 2 1/2 cups of batter into a small bowl. Whisk in cocoa powder. Alternately spoon vanilla and chocolate batters into prepared tube pan. Using a knife, cut and twist through batter to create a marble effect.

Bake 60 minutes or until a toothpick comes out clean. Cool in pan on a wire rack for 10 minutes. Then run a spatula or knife around the pan to loosen the cake. Remove cake and cook on a wire rack.

Coconut Cake

¾ pound (3 sticks) unsalted butter, softened
2 cups sugar
6 large eggs (crack eggs in a small bowl)
1 ½ tsp pure vanilla extract
1 ½ tsp pure almond extract
1 ½ tsp coconut flavor
3 cups all-purpose flour, sifted
1 ¼ tsp baking powder
½ tsp baking soda
½ tsp kosher salt
1 (8 ounce) can coconut milk
4 ounces sweetened shredded coconut

Preheat oven to 350 degrees .Grease and flour 3 8-inch round cake pans, then lined then lined them parchment paper.

In the bowl of an electric mixer fitted with a paddle attachment, cream the butter and sugar on medium-high speed for 3 to 5 minutes, until light yellow and fluffy. With the mixer on medium speed, add the eggs 1 at a time, scrapping down the bowl once during mixing. Add the vanilla, almond and coconut flavorings and mix well. The mixture might look curdled, don't worry.

In a separate bowl, sift together the flour, baking powder, baking soda and salt. With the mixer on low speed, alternately add the dry ingredients and the milk to the batter in 3 parts, beginning and ending with dry ingredients. Mix until just combined. Fold in the ½ cup shredded coconut with a rubber spatula.

Pour the batter evenly into the pans and smooth the top with a knife. Bake in the center of the oven for 45 to 55 minutes, until the top are browned and a cake tester comes out clean. Cool on a baking rack for 30 minutes, then turn the cakes out onto a baking rack to finish cooling.

<u>Frosting</u>
1 pound cream cheese, softened
1 cup (2 sticks) unsalted butter, softened
¾ tsp pure vanilla extract
¼ tsp pure almond extract

1 pound plus 1 cup confectioners' sugar, sifted
½ cup sweetened shredded coconut
½ cup toasted sweetened shredded coconut

In the bowl of an electric mixer fitted with a paddle attachment, combine the cream cheese, butter, vanilla and almond extract on low speed. Add the sifted confectioners' sugar and mix until just smooth. Begin layering the cake to frost.

Cream Cheese Pound Cake

1 ½ cups softened unsalted butter
1 (8 ounce) softened package cream cheese
3 ¼ cups sugar
6 large eggs
3 cups all-purpose flour, sifted
Dash of kosher salt
2 ½ tsp vanilla

Preheat oven to 325 degrees.

Beat softened butter and cream cheese at medium speed with an electric mixer about 2 to 3 minutes or until creamy. Gradually add sugar, beating 5 to 7 minutes. Add eggs, 1 at a time, beating just until yellow disappears. Gradually add sifted flour mixture, mixing at low speed just until blended; hand stir in vanilla.

Pour into greased and floured 10-inch tube pan. Bake at 325 degrees for 1 ½ hours or until a wooden toothpick or cake tester inserted in center of cake comes out clean.

Cool in pan 10 minutes; remove cake from pan, and cool completely on a wire rack.

German Chocolate Cake

Four 8-inch round layers
3 cups sifted cake flour
1 ¼ tsp baking soda
½ tsp kosher salt
5 ounces sweet baking chocolate, finely chopped
½ cup boiling water
2 tsp vanilla
1 ¼ cup buttermilk
1 cup (2 sticks) plus 1 tbsp. unsalted butter, softened
2 cups sugar
5 large eggs separated
¼ tsp cream of tartar
¼ cup sugar

Preheat oven to 350 degrees F. Grease and flour four 8x2 inch round cake pans lined the bottoms with parchment paper.

Whisk together cake flour, baking soda and salt until thoroughly blended. Combine baking chocolate and boiling water until the chocolate is melted and smooth, stir in vanilla. Mix butter until creamy, about 30 to 45 seconds. Gradually add sugar and beat on high speed until light and fluffy, 5 – 7 minutes. Beat eggs yolks in one at a time. On low speed, add the melted chocolate and beat just until incorporated. Add the flour mixture in 3 parts, alternating with the buttermilk in 2 parts, beating until smooth and scraping the sides of the bowl with a rubber spatula as necessary.

Using clean beaters, in a large bowl beat egg whites and cream of tartar on medium speed until soft peaks form. Gradually add sugar, beating on high speed. Beat until the peaks are stiff. Use a rubber spatula to fold one-quarter of the egg whites into the egg yolk mixture, then fold in the remaining whites. Divide the batter among the pans and spread evenly.

Bake until a toothpick or cake tester inserted in center comes out clean, 30 to 35 minutes. Cool cakes on racks for 30 minutes.

Coconut Frosting

- 1 cup sugar
- 3 egg yolks
- 1 tsp pure vanilla extract
- 1 cup chopped pecans
- ½ cup (1 stick) unsalted butter, softened
- 1 can condensed milk
- 1 tbsp. cornstarch
- 2 cups sweetened dried coconut

Combine ingredients and cook over low heat; stirring constantly until thickened, about 10-12 minutes. Gradually add all chopped pecans and coconut.

Chocolate Frosting (sides of cake)

Melt in the top of a double boiler or a heatproof bowl the following ingredients:
- 3 ounces unsweetened chocolate, coarsely chopped
- 3 tbsp. unsalted butter

Remove from the heat and stir in:
- ½ cup hot coffee and cream
- 1 tsp vanilla
- 1 tsp chocolate imitation flavor

Gradually add, beating until spreadable:
- 2 to 2 ½ cups confectioners' sugar, sifted

Golden Citrus Cake

3 cups sifted cake flour
3 tsp baking powder
¼ tsp kosher salt
8 large egg yolks
1 ½ tsp pure vanilla extract
1 tsp grated lemon zest
1 tsp fresh lemon juice
¾ cup (1 ½ stick) soften unsalted butter
1 ½ cups sugar
1 cup whole milk

Preheat oven to 350 degrees. Grease and flour three 9x2 inch round cake pans. Whisk together cake flour, baking powder and salt thoroughly. Beat egg yolks, vanilla, lemon zest and lemon juice in a large bowl until thick and lemon colored. In a separate bowl beat butter until creamy. Gradually add sugar and beat on high speed until light and fluffy, 3 to 5 minutes. Beat in the yolk mixture. On low speed, add the flour mixture in 3 parts, alternating with milk. In 2 parts, beating until smooth. Divide the batter among the pans and spread evenly. Bake until cake wooden pick or cake tester inserted into the center comes out clean, 18 to 21 minutes. Cool the cakes completely out of the pan, on a rack.

<u>Orange Custard Filling</u>

Whisk together in a medium saucepan until well blended:
    1/3 cup sugar
    1/3 tsp all-purpose flour
    Dash kosher salt
    1 cup whole milk (Mix in until smooth)

Whisk in:
    ½ cup fresh orange juice
    1 tsp orange zest

Cook over medium heat, whisking constantly until the mixture comes out a boil and then continue to cook, whisking briskly, minute. Remove from heat.

Whisk in a small bowl until frothy:
>   1 egg

Whisk about a one-third of the sauce into the egg. Return this mixture to the pan. Continue to cook, whisking, until the filling begins to simmer and thickens. Let cool, cover, and refrigerate to thicken.

<u>Frosting</u>
>   ½ cup softened unsalted butter
>   6 cups confectioners' sifted sugar
>   5 to 8 tbsp. fresh orange juice
>   Grated zest of a small orange

Mix until well blended and spread frosting on the cake.

Red Velvet

2 ¼ cups all-purpose flour
1 teaspoon of baking soda
1 ¼ teaspoon of baking powder
1 teaspoon of salt
2 tbsp. unsweetened Gourmet cocoa powder
2 cups sugar
1/2 cup vegetable oil
1 stick butter
2 eggs
1 ¼ cup buttermilk
2 tsp pure vanilla extract
2 oz. red food coloring
1 teaspoon of white distilled vinegar
½ cup of prepared Red Velvet Flavored brewed hot coffee (don't skip this ingredient)

Preheat oven to 325 degrees. In a large bowl, combine the sugar and vegetable oil.

Mix in the eggs, buttermilk, vanilla and red food coloring until combined.

Stir in the coffee (room temperature) and white vinegar. Combine the wet ingredients with the dry ingredients a little at time, mixing after each addition, just until combined.

Generously grease and flour two round, 9 inch cake pans with shortening and flour.

Pour the batter evenly into each pan.

Bake in the middle rack for 30-40 minutes, or until a toothpick comes out clean. Do not over bake as cake will continue to cook as it cools. Let cool on a cooling rack until the pans are warm to the touch. Slide a knife or offset spatula around the inside of the pans to loosen the cake from the pan.

Remove the cakes from the pan and let them cool. Frost the cake with cream cheese frosting when the cakes have cooled completely.

Frosting

    8 cups confectioners' sugar, sifted
    1 8-ounce cream cheese, softened
    1 cup (½ stick butter) unsalted, softened
    1 tsp pure vanilla extract

Place softened butter in the bowl of the electric mixer and cream smooth, transfer to a separate bowl and reserve. Place room temperature cream cheese in the bowl of the electric mixer and smooth, but do not whip or beat on high speed. Add the reserved butter to the cream cheese and mix together until smooth. Add sifted confectioner's sugar all at once, mix just until blended. Add the vanilla extract. Spread frosting on cake.

Vanilla Cake

12 tbsp. (1 ½ sticks) unsalted butter, softened
1 ½ cups sugar
2 ¼ cups cake flour
1 package of instant vanilla pudding
2 tsp baking powder
¼ tsp kosher salt
6 large egg whites (¾ cup)
1 ¼ cup whole milk
2 tsp pure vanilla extract
1 tbsp. vanilla beans
2 tsp almond extract

Set Rack at the middle level in the oven and preheat to 350 degrees F.

Brush shortening in bottom and around the sides followed by dusting flour on two 9 inch or one 13x9x2 pan. In a large bowl, sift flour, baking powder, salt and instant pudding together and set aside. In a second large bowl, beat butter and sugar for about 5 minutes, until light and fluffy. Combine egg whites, milk, vanilla and almond extract. Add 1/3 of the flour mixture to the butter/egg mixture then add half of the milk mixture. Continue to alternate beginning and ending with flour mixture. Scrape the bowl and beater often.

Pour the batter into prepared pans (s) and smooth top with a metal spatula. Bake cake (s) about 25 to 30 minutes, or until toothpick inserted in the center emerges clean.

Glaze
    2 tbsp. confectioners' sugar
    2 tsp pure vanilla beans
    1 tsp pure vanilla extract
    1 tbsp. milk (add a little at a time if you need more)

Whisk together, set aside. Cool in pan for 5 minutes, turn out onto a rack, while cake (s) are warm, and brush glaze on the cakes

Frosting
- 1 cup unsalted butter (2 sticks), softened
- 3 – 4 cups confectioners' sugar, sifted
- 1 tbsp. powder meringue
- 1 tbsp. vanilla bean extract
- Up to 4 tablespoons milk or heavy cream

Beat butter for a few minutes with a mixer with the paddle attachment on medium speed. Sift powdered sugar and meringue together. Add 3 cups of powdered sugar and meringue turn your mixer on the lowest speed (so the sugar doesn't blow everywhere) until the sugar has been incorporated with the butter. Increase mixer speed to medium and add vanilla bean extract, and 2 tablespoons of milk/cream and beat for 3 minutes. If your frosting needs a more stiff consistency, add remaining sugar. If your frosting needs to be thinned out, add remaining milk 1 tablespoons at a time.

Lemon Pound Cake

3 sticks plus 1 tsp unsalted butter, at room temperature
2 ½ cups sugar
5 eggs (only use 2 yolks of the 5 eggs)
2 tbsp. lemon zest
4 tbsp. freshly squeezed lemon juice
3 cups sifted cake flour (sift 3 times)
1 ½ tsp baking powder
1 tsp kosher salt
1-4 ounce Lemon Instant Pudding Mix
1 ½ cup milk, in a separate cup add 2 more tbsp., at room temperature
1 tsp pure vanilla extract
2 ½ cups confectioner's sugar, sifted

Heat oven to 350 degrees F. Grease and flour 2 loaf pans or 1-bundt pan. Sift flour, baking powder and salt. After sifting add lemon instant pudding, sit aside.

Cream butter (3 sticks only) for 5 minutes, add sugar and mix together until light and fluffy. Mixing at medium speed, add eggs one at a time; add lemon zest and 2 tbsp. lemon juice

Add flour mixture and milk alternately to butter and sugar mixture

Add vanilla extract. Pour batter into desired pans, smoothing tops, and bake at 345 degrees for 45 minutes to 60 minutes, until cake tester comes out clean.

When cake is done, let it cool for 5 minutes onto a rack or a cookie sheet or parchment paper (for easier clean up).

<u>Glaze</u>

Combine confectioner's sugar, 2 tbsp. milk, 1 tsp butter and remaining lemon juice, mix until smooth. While cake is still warm, spoon glaze on cake; wait 5 minutes, pour remaining glaze to drizzle down the sides.

Chocolate Buttermilk Cake

    1 cup butter
    2 ¼ cups sugar
    2 eggs
    1 tsp pure vanilla extract
    ½ cup cocoa
    3 cups sifted cake flour
    2 tsp baking powder
    1 tsp kosher salt
    2 cups buttermilk
    ¼ cup room temperature coffee

Cream softened butter until smooth; add sugar gradually and beat until fluffy. Add eggs one at a time. Add coffee to buttermilk. Add sifted dry ingredients to creamed mixture alternately with buttermilk mixture. Pour batter into three greased, waxed paper lined pans.

Bake 25 to 30 minutes at 350 degrees. Cool completely before frosting.

<u>Cream Cheese Frosting</u>
    1 (8 ounce) square Philadelphia cream cheese
    ½ cup unsalted butter
    6 cups sifted confectioner sugar
    1 tsp vanilla
    3 tbsp.

Place softened butter in the bowl of the electric mixer and cream smooth, transfer to a separate bowl and reserve. Place room temperature cream cheese in the bowl of the electric mixer and smooth, but do not whip or beat on high speed. Add the reserved butter to the cream cheese and mix together until smooth. Add sifted confectioner's sugar and cocoa powder all at once, mix just until blended. Add the vanilla extract. Spread frosting on cake.

Sock-It-To-Me Bundt Cake

1 box yellow cake mix, butter recipe
½ cup sugar
1 cup sour cream
¾ cup vegetable oil
1 tsp butternut imitation flavor
2 tsp butter imitation flavor
4 eggs

<u>Cinnamon Mixture</u>
4 tbsp. packed dark brown sugar
2 tsp sugar
2 tsp ground cinnamon

Preheat oven to 325 degrees F. Grease and flour 1 12-cup tubed cake pan. In a small bowl, stir cinnamon mixture ingredients. In large bowl, beat cake ingredients with electric mixer on medium speed until well blended. Spread half of batter in pan. Sprinkle cinnamon mixture over batter, pour remaining batter over top of cinnamon mixture.

Bake 55-60 minutes. Cool in pan 5 to 8 minutes. Run knife around edge and center of pan. Place cooling rack upside down over pan; turn rack and pan over.

<u>Vanilla Glaze</u>
1 cup confectioners' sugar
1 tbsp. clear vanilla flavor
1 tsp. milk

Whisk ingredients until well blended and pour over cake.

Sour Cream Pound Cake

1 cup softened unsalted butter
3 cups sugar
6 large eggs
3 cups all-purpose flour, sifted
¼ tsp baking soda
1 (8 ounce) carton sour cream (do not use fat free)
2 tsp pure vanilla extract

Preheat oven to 325 Degrees. Beat butter at medium speed with an electric mixer about 2 to 3 minutes or until creamy. Gradually add sugar, beating at medium speed 5 to 7 minutes. Add eggs, 1 at a time, beating just until yellow disappears.

Gradually add sifted flour mixture to butter mixture alternately with sour cream, beginning and ending with flour mixture. Mix at low speed just until blended after each addition. Stir in vanilla. Pour batter into a greased and floured 12-cup Bundt or 10- inch tube pan.

Bake at 325 degrees for 1 ½ hours or until a wooden pick or cake tester inserted in center of cake comes out clean. Cool in pan on a wire rack 10 to 15 minutes; remove from pan, and cool on wire rack.

<u>Variation:</u> Separate eggs; add yolks to batter, beating until blended. Stir in sour cream and vanilla. Beat egg whites until stiff, and fold into batter. Spoon into prepared pan, bake as directed

Strawberry Sour Cream Pound Cake

1 cup butter, softened
3 cups sugar
4 large eggs
3 cups sifted cake flour
¼ tsp baking soda
¼ tsp kosher salt
1 (8 ounce) carton sour cream
1 tsp vanilla extract
1 tsp orange extract
1 tsp lemon extract
1/3 cup strawberry puree

Beat butter at medium speed with an electric mixer 5-7 minutes or until creamy. Gradually add sugar, beating at medium speed 5-7 minutes.

Separate eggs; add yolks to batter, beating until blended. Combine flour, baking soda and salt; gradually add to egg and butter mixture alternately with sour cream, beginning and ending with flour mixture; and vanilla, lemon and orange extract. Beat egg whites until stiff, and fold into batter. Fold strawberry puree into the batter. Pour batter into a greased and floured 12-cup Bundt or 10-inch tube pan.

Bake at 325 for 1 ½ hours or until a wooden pick inserted in center of cake comes out clean. Cool in pan on a wire rack 10 – 15 minutes; remove from pan and cool on wire rack.

<u>Glaze</u>
    2 cups confectioner sugar
    1 tsp water

Whisk together until well blended and pour over warm cake.

Key Lime Cake

    1 package lemon cake mix
    1 1/3 cups vegetable oil
    4 eggs
    1 (3 ounce) package lime flavored Jell-O mix
    ½ cup orange juice
    5 tbsp. lime juice
    1 (8 ounce) package cream cheese, softened
    1 (3 ounce) package cream cheese, softened
    6 cups confectioners' sugar, sifted

Grease and flour 3 8-inch round cake pans. Combine cake mix, gelatin mix, oil, eggs, orange juice and lime juice. Pour into prepared pans. Bake according to instructions on box of cake mix. Drizzle glaze on hot cakes, allow to cool completely before frosting.

<u>Glaze</u>
    1 cup confectioners' sugar
    1 tbsp. lime juice

Whisk together until well blended.

<u>Cream Cheese Frosting</u>
    ½ cup butter (1 stick) unsalted, softened
    1 (8-ounce) package cream cheese, softened
    3 cups sifted confectioners' sugar
    ½ tsp lime juice
    1 tbsp. lime zest

Beat butter and cream cheese at medium speed with an electric mixer until creamy. Add powdered sugar and lime juice and lime zest, beat until smooth. Spread frosting on the cake.

Classic Cheesecake

    4 (8-ounce) cream cheese, softened
    1 ½ cup sugar
    1 cup sour cream, room temperature
    2 tbsp. cornstarch
    2 tsp pure vanilla extract
    1 tsp lemon extract
    4 eggs, lightly beaten

<u>Crust</u>
    2 cups graham cracker crumbs
    1/3 cup butter, melted
    2 tbsp. sugar
    ¼ tsp almond extract

Mix graham cracker crumbs with butter, sugar and almond extract. Press into bottom and up sides of pan. Place pan into the freezer for 20 minutes.

Cream cheese until creamy, add sugar, beating until fully incorporated. Beat in sour cream, cornstarch, vanilla and lemon flavoring, scraping down sides. Beat in eggs only until fully combined, do not over mix. Remove pan from freezer, pour batter into crust.

Bake in oven at 400 degrees F for 15 minutes. Reduce heat to 225 degrees F. Continue to bake for 1 hour. Run knife around edge of cake to loosen cheesecake. Turn off oven; leave cake in oven with door slightly ajar, 1 hour. Remove cake from oven, cool on a wire rack; let cake cool completely. Refrigerate, uncovered, at least 6 hours or overnight.

Top cake with your favorite fruit.

Devil's Food Cheesecake

3 (8-ounce) package cream cheese, at room temperature
1 ½ cups sugar
3 tbsp. cornstarch
1 ½ tbsp. pure vanilla extract
3 large eggs
2/3 cup heavy or whipping cream

<u>Devil's Food Cake</u>
2 ½ cups sifted cake flour
2 ¼ tsp baking powder
½ tsp kosher salt
¾ cup (1 ½ sticks) unsalted butter, at room temperature
1 cup sugar
½ cup firmly packed dark brown sugar
4 large eggs, separated
5 ounces bittersweet or semisweet chocolate, melted and cooled
1 tbsp. pure vanilla extract
1 tbsp. chocolate imitation flavor
1 ½ cups whole milk
½ teaspoon cream of tartar

<u>Frosting</u>
8 cups sifted confectioner's sugar
¾ cup unsweetened cocoa powder
½ tsp kosher salt
2 cups (4 sticks) unsalted butter, at room temperature
7 ounces bittersweet or semisweet chocolate, melted and cooled
2 tbsp. dark corn syrup
2 tbsp. pure vanilla extract
¾ cup heavy or whipping cream

Early in the day, preheat the oven to 350 degrees and generously butter the bottom and sides of one 9-inch spring form pan. Wrap the outside of the pan with foil, covering the bottom and sides.

<u>Cheesecake:</u> To make the cheesecake layer, put one package of the cream cheese, 1/3 cup of sugar, and the cornstarch in a large bowl and beat with an electric mixer on low until creamy, about 3 minutes, scraping down the

bowl a couple of times. Blend in the remaining cream cheese one at a time, scraping down the bowl after each. Increase the mixer speed to medium and beat in the remaining sugar, then the vanilla. Blend in the eggs, one at a time beating well after adding each. Beat in the cream just until it's completely blended. Be careful not to over mix!

Gently spoon the batter into the foil-wrapped spring form pan and place it in a large shallow pan containing hot water that comes about 1 inch up the sides of the pan. Bake the cake at 350 degrees F until the edges are light golden brown and the top is slightly golden tan, about 1 ¼ hours. Remove the cake from the water bath, transfer to a wire rack, and cool in the pan for 2 hours covered with plastic wrap, and refrigerate (while still in the pan) until it's completely cold, about 4 hours. Place in the freezer until ready to assemble the cake.

Remove water bath; check temperature oven. Oven temperature should be 350 degrees. Generously butter the bottom and sides of three 9-inch round layer cake pans. Line the bottom of all three pans with parchment paper (very important step).

<u>Devil's Food Cake</u>: Sift the flour, baking powder and salt in a bowl. Cream the butter and both sugars together in a large bowl with the mixer on medium until light yellow and creamy. Add the egg yolks, one at a time, beating well after each. Beat in the melted chocolate, vanilla and chocolate flavoring. Using a wooden spoon, stir in the flour mixture, alternately with the milk, mixing well after each until blended.

Combine the egg whites and cream of tartar in a clean medium-size bowl and beat with clean, dry beaters on high until stiff peaks form. Fold about one-third of the whites into the chocolate batter until they disappear, then gently fold in the remaining whites. Don't worry if you still see a few white specks, they'll disappear during baking. Divide the batter evenly between the three pans. Bake until a toothpick or cake tester inserted in the centers comes out with moist crumbs cling to it, about 30 minutes. Cool the cakes in the pans on a rack for 15 minutes, then remove the cakes from the pans and gently peel off the paper liners. Let cool completely, about 2 hours, then cover with plastic wrap and refrigerate overnight or until ready to assemble the cake.

Frosting

In a large bowl, sift confectioners' sugar, cocoa, and salt together. In another large bowl, cream the butter with a mixer on high until light yellow and slightly thickened, about 3 minutes. With the mixer still running, beat in the chocolate, corn syrup and vanilla. Reduce the mixer speed to low and beat in the sugar cocoa mixture in two additions, beating well after each. Blend in the cream until the frosting is spreading consistency, adding a little more cream if needed. Whip the frosting on high until light and creamy, about 2 minutes more.

To assemble the cake, remove the cheesecake from the freezer and let stand at room temperature about 10 minutes. Place one layer of devil's food cake, top side down, on a cake plate and spread with some of the frosting. Remove cake from the spring form pan, place top side down on the frosted cake layer and spread with some frosting. Top with a second devil's food layer, top side down. Spread with more frosting and cover with the third devil's food layer, top side up. Brush away any crumbs from the sides and top of the fudge cake layers. Frost the sides and top of the cake with the remaining frosting, spreading the top with frosting about ½ inch deep. Use a long metal spatula that has been warmed under hot running water to smooth out the frosting on the sides and top of the cake. With a small spatula or table knife, swirl the frosting on top into a decorative design.

Refrigerate the cake for at least 2 hours to allow the cheesecake to thaw.

Oreo Cheesecake

6 tbsp. unsalted softened butter
One 9-ounce package chocolate wafer cookies, finely crushed (about 2 cups)
1 cup crushed whole Oreo cookies
2 ¼ cups sugar
3 tbsp. sugar
4 (8-ounce packages) softened cream cheese
3 tbsp. cornstarch
1 cup sour cream, room temperature
1 ½ tsp pure vanilla extract
5 large eggs

Preheat oven to 350 degrees. Butter the sides of a 10-inch spring form pan. Double wrap exterior of pan (including base) in foil. Melt 6 tablespoons butter in a small saucepan over medium heat. Place crushed wafer cookies and 3 tablespoons sugar in a large bowl; stir until well combined. Pour melted butter over cookies mixture and mix until evenly moistened. Press mixture evenly into the bottom of the prepared pan.

Place pan on a baking sheet. Bake until crust is set, 9 to 11 minutes. Transfer pan to a wire rack to cool completely.

In the bow of an electric mixer fitted with the paddle attachment, beat the cream cheese on medium speed until fluffy, about 3 minutes, scraping down sides as needed. In a large bowl, whisk together remaining 2 ¼ cups sugar and cornstarch. With mixer on low speed, gradually add sugar mixture to cream cheese; mix until smooth. Add sour cream and vanilla; mix until smooth. Add eggs, one at a time, beating until just combined; do not overmix.

Slightly fold crushed Oreo cookies into mixture.

Pour cream cheese filling into prepared pan. Set pan inside a large, shallow roasting pan. Carefully ladle boiling water into roasting pan to reach halfway up sides of spring form pan. Bake 45 minutes; reduce oven temperature to 325 degrees. Continue baking until cake is set but still slightly wobbly in the center, about 30 minutes more. Turn off oven, leave cake in over with door slightly ajar, 1 hour. Transfer pan to a wire rack; let cake cool completely.

Refrigerate, uncovered, at least 6 hours or overnight. Before unmolding, run a knife around the edge of the cake.

Pies, Puddings
&
Other Baked Breads

Sweet Potato Pie

4 cups mashed sweet potatoes
3 brown eggs
1/2 cup carnation milk or light whipping cream
1 cup unsalted butter
1 tsp kosher salt
1 tsp grated lemon zest
1 tsp vanilla
1 tsp nutmeg
2 unbaked 2 inch pie shells (I prefer Ritz)

Boil or bake potatoes in skin until soft. While potatoes are cooking, line crust edge with aluminum foil to avoid burning.

Beat potatoes before adding any ingredients to separate the strings. Add butter and mix well. Add 6 remaining ingredients. Beat on medium speed until mixture is smooth. Pour into pie shells.

Bake at 350 degrees for 55-60 minutes or knife inserted in center comes out clean.

Coconut Cream Pie

One 9-inch single-crust pie
2/3 cup sugar
½ cup cornstarch
¼ tsp salt
2 cups whole milk
½ cup canned coconut milk
5 large egg yolks
3 tbsp. unsalted butter, cut into small pieces
1 ½ tsp pure vanilla extract
½ tsp coconut flavor
1 ½ cup shredded sweetened dried coconut, toasted

Whisk sugar, cornstarch and salt in a medium heavy saucepan until well blended. Gradually whisk in whole and coconut milk

Vigorously whisk in eggs yolks until no yellow streaks remain. Stirring constantly medium heat. Remove from the heat, scrape the corners of the saucepan, and whisk until smooth. Return to the head and, whisking constantly, bring to a simmer and cook for 60 to 70 seconds. Remove pan from heat and whisk in butter, vanilla and coconut flavor.

Spoon the filling into prepared crust and press a sheet of plastic wrap directly on the surface.

<u>Soft meringue topping</u>
1 tbsp. cornstarch
1 tbsp. sugar
1/3 cup water
5 egg whites
½ tsp vanilla
¼ tsp cream of tartar

Mix cornstarch and sugar thoroughly in a small saucepan. Gradually stir in water making a smooth, runny paste. Bring to a boil over medium heat, stirring briskly all the while, then boil for 15 to 17 seconds. Remove the thick paste from the heat and cover. Beat in a clean grease-free glass or metal bowl until foamy. Add egg whites beat until soft peaks from. Very gradually beat in remaining sugar.

Beat on high speed until the peaks are very stiff and glossy but not dry. Reduce speed to very low and beat in the cornstarch paste 1 tablespoon at a time. When all the paste is incorporated, increase the speed to medium and beat for 10 to 12 seconds.

Spread over a hot pie filling, bake the pie at 350 degrees F for 20 minutes, let cool completely on a rack, then refrigerate. Before serving sprinkle toasted coconut flakes (optional).

Easy Peach Cobbler

Two 15-ounce cans sliced peaches in syrup
1/2 cup (1 stick) butter
1 cup self-rising flour
(Can substitute self-rising flour with 1 cup all-purpose flour mixed with 1 tbsp. baking powder and 1/8 teaspoon salt)
1 cup sugar
1 cup whole milk

Preheat the oven to 350 degrees. Drain 1 can of peaches; reserve the syrup from the other. Place the butter in a 9- by 12-inch ovenproof baking dish.

Heat the butter on the stove or in the oven until it's melted. In a medium bowl, mix the flour and sugar. Stir in the milk and the reserved syrup. Pour the batter over the melted butter in the baking dish. Arrange the peaches over the batter. Bake for 1 hour.

The cobbler is done when the batter rises around the peaches and the crust is thick and golden brown.

Key Lime Pie

One 15-ounce can sweetened condensed milk
4 large egg yolks
½ cup Key lime juice (12-14 key limes) or ½ cup Nellie's Key Lime Juice
4 tsp grated key lime zest

Whisk together until well blended. Pour the filling into the piecrust of your choosing.

<u>Soft meringue topping</u>
   1 tbsp. cornstarch
   1 tbsp. sugar
   1/3 cup water
   4 egg whites
   ½ tsp pure vanilla extract
   ¼ tsp cream of tartar

Mix cornstarch and sugar thoroughly in a small saucepan. Gradually stir in water making a smooth, runny paste. Bring to a boil over medium heat, stirring briskly all the while, then boil for 15 to 17 seconds. Remove the thick paste from the heat and cover. Beat in a clean grease-free glass or metal bowl until foamy. Add egg whites beat until soft peaks from. Very gradually bean in remaining sugar. Beat on high speed until the peaks are very stiff and glossy but not dry. Reduce speed to very low and beat in the cornstarch paste 1 tablespoon at a time. When all the paste is incorporated, increase the speed to medium and beat for 10 to 12 seconds.

Spread over a hot pie filling, bake the pie at 325 degrees F for 20 minutes, let cool completely on a rack, then refrigerate.

Before serving sprinkle thin almond slices (optional).

Lemon Meringue Pie

½ recipe deluxe butter pie or pastry dough
½ cups sugar
6 tbsp. cornstarch
¼ tsp salt
½ cup cold water
½ cup fresh lemon juice or Nellie's Lemon Juice
3 egg yolks, well beaten
2 tbsp. unsalted butter, cut into small pieces
1 ½ cups boiling water
1 ¼ tsp grated lemon zest

Line a 9-inch pie pan with deluxe butter pie or pastry dough. Combine sugar, cornstarch and salt in a 2-3 quart saucepan. Gradually blend in water, lemon juice. Add egg yolks blending thoroughly. Add butter stirring constantly and gradually add boiling water, stirring gently. Once it begins to thicken, reduce the heat and simmer slowly 1 minute. Remove from heat and stir in lemon zest.

<u>Soft meringue topping</u>
    1 tbsp. cornstarch
    1 tbsp. sugar
    1/3 cup water
    3 egg whites
    ½ tsp vanilla
    ¼ tsp cream of tartar

Mix cornstarch and sugar thoroughly in a small saucepan. Gradually stir in water making a smooth, runny paste. Bring to a boil over medium heat, stirring briskly all the while, then boil for 15 to 17 seconds. Remove the thick paste from the heat and cover. Beat in a clean grease-free glass or metal bowl until foamy. Add egg whites beat until soft peaks from. Very gradually beat in remaining sugar. Beat on high speed until the peaks are very stiff and glossy but not dry. Reduce speed to very low and beat in the cornstarch paste 1 tablespoon at a time. When all the paste is incorporated, increase the speed to medium and beat for 10 to 12 seconds.

Spread over a hot pie filling, bake the pie for 20 minutes, let cool completely on a rack, then refrigerate.

Banana Pudding

Part I
    4 large eggs
    ¾ cup sugar
    3 tbsp. all-purpose flour
    ½ tsp plus a dash salt
    2 cups whole milk
    ½ tsp pure vanilla extract
    ½ tsp banana imitation flavor
    1 (16 ounce) plus 1 cup crushed package vanilla wafers

Separate the yolks from the whites of 3 of the eggs; set aside the whites. Add the remaining whole egg to the yolks.

In saucepan, whisk together ½ cup sugar, the flour and ½ tsp sale. Stir in the whole egg and 3 yolks, and then stir in the milk. Cook uncovered, stirring often, until the mixture thickens, about 10 minutes. Remove from the heat and stir in the vanilla and banana flavorings.

Spread a thin layer of the cooked pudding in a 1 ½ or larger casserole dish. Arrange a layer of vanilla wafers on top of the pudding. Thinly slice the bananas crosswise, about 1/8 inch thick, and arrange a layer of banana slices over the wafers. Spread one-third of the remaining pudding over the bananas and continue layering wafers, bananas and pudding ending with pudding. Set pudding aside to completely cool.

Part II
    Cool Whip Topping
    1 (5 ounce) package instant banana pudding mix
    2 cups cold milk
    1 tsp pure vanilla extract
    1 (12 ounce) container frozen whipped topping, thawed

In a large mixing bowl, beat pudding mix and milk 2 minutes. Stir in vanilla and fold in whipped topping. Set aside to spread over cooked cooled pudding. Sprinkle crushed vanilla wafers over the chilled cool whipped pudding.

Bread Pudding

2 large tart apples or pears (fruit is optional)
1 cup raisins
2 cups sugar
5 large beaten eggs
1 tbsp. ground cinnamon
1 cup packed light brown sugar
¼ cup (1/2 stick) unsalted butter, softened
½ cup pecan pieces
2 cups whole milk
2 tsp pure vanilla extract
¼ tsp ground nutmeg
8 to 10 slices of stale Egg bread, or French bread or Panettone bread

Preheat oven to 350 degrees. Grease a 2 quart baking dish. Peel, core and slice apples or pears. In a small saucepan combine fruit slices and ¼ cup water. Bring to boiling, reduce heat. Cook, covered over medium-low heat for 5 to 7 minutes or till slices are tender, stirring occasionally. Drain in colander. Transfer fruit slices to a small bowl. Gently stir cinnamon into cook fruit slices. Set Aside.

Mix together eggs, milk, sugar, cinnamon (if not using fruit) pecans and vanilla. Place half 4 to 5 slices bread in baking dish. Place fruit slices and raisins over bread. Place the remaining slices of bread over fruit. Pour Egg mixture over all. Bake for 35 to 45 minutes or until set.

<u>Sauce</u>
1 cup sugar
½ cup (1 stick) unsalted butter
1 egg, beaten
2 tsp pure vanilla extract

Mix together sugar, butter, egg and vanilla in a saucepan over medium heat. Stir together until the sugar is melted. Pour over bread pudding.

Banana Bread

1 ½ cup all-purpose flour
1 ½ tsp baking powder
½ tsp apple allspice
1 tsp cinnamon
½ tsp kosher salt
½ cup light brown sugar
½ cup granulated sugar
6 tbsp. of unsalted butter, softened
1 tsp coconut butter
¾ tsp grated lemon zest
½ tsp pure vanilla extract
2 large eggs, beaten
2 to 3 ripe bananas (mashed)
½ cup chopped nuts – optional

Preheat oven to 350 degrees. Grease an 8 ½ x 4 ½ inch loaf pan. Whisk together flour, baking powder and salt, cinnamon, apple all-spice. Beat in a large bowl at medium speed until creamy, unsalted butter, coconut butter, and lemon zest. Beat in, eggs and mashed bananas. Stir in vanilla extract and nuts (optional).

Scrape the batter into the greased pan. Bank the bread about 1 hour, or until a toothpick inserted in the center comes out clean. Cool slightly, then unmold. Cool completely before slicing.

Buttermilk Biscuits

2 cups all-purpose flour, plus extra for dusting
2 tbsp. Bisquick mix
¼ tsp baking soda
1 ½ tbsp. baking powder
1 tsp kosher salt
6 tbsp. unsalted cold butter
3 tbsp. of cold shortening
1 tbsp. of cold coconut oil
1 cup buttermilk

Preheat oven to 450 degrees F.

Sift together flour, baking powder and salt. Cut in, using a pastry blender or 2 knives, until the size of small peas. Make a well in the center. Add ¾ cup buttermilk. Stir just until the dough comes away from the sides of the bowl. Turn the dough out onto a lightly floured board. Knead gently and quickly, about 8 to 10 times. Roll out with a lightly floured rolling pin, to between ¼ and ½ inch thick. Cut with a 1 ½ inch biscuit cutter dipped in very little flour, and place on an ungreased baking sheet. Brush the tops with milk or melted butter. Bake until lightly browned, 12 – 15 minutes.

Southern Cornbread

4 tbsp. bacon fat
3 tbsp. unsalted butter
2 cups self-rising cornmeal
3 tbsp. self-rising flour
3 tbsp. sugar
3 large eggs, slightly beaten
2 ½ cups buttermilk, room temperature

Preheat oven to 450 degrees. In a heavy oven-proof skillet, preferably cast iron, or glass baking dish add the bacon drippings and the butter.

Whisk together cornmeal, flour and sugar. Add eggs and buttermilk to dry ingredients, beat until well blended. Remove pan from oven, pour bacon drippings and butter into batter, mix until blended. Pour batter into hot baking dish; bake until the top is browned and the center feels frim when pressed, 20 to 25 minutes.

Brush melted butter over warm bread, cut into wedges or squares.

www.ingramcontent.com/pod-product-compliance
Lightning Source LLC
Chambersburg PA
CBHW070624300426
44113CB00010B/1652